No
More
Push
Parenting

How to Find Success and Balance
in a Hypercompetitive World

No
More
Push
Parenting

ELISABETH GUTHRIE, M.D.,
AND KATHY MATTHEWS

BROADWAY BOOKS   NEW YORK

BROADWAY

While the personal stories in this book are drawn from Dr. Elisabeth Guthrie's experiences, all names and identifying details have been changed to protect the confidentiality of her patients. In some cases, composites have been drawn from experiences with several children.

A hardcover edition of this book, formerly titled *The Trouble with Perfect*, was published in 2002 by Broadway Books.

Broadway Books titles may be purchased for business or promotional use or for special sales. For information, please write to: Special Markets Department, Random House, Inc., 1745 Broadway, New York, NY 10019.

PRINTED IN THE UNITED STATES OF AMERICA

BROADWAY BOOKS and its logo, a letter B bisected on the diagonal, are trademarks of Broadway Books, a division of Random House, Inc.

Visit our website at www.broadwaybooks.com

First Broadway Books trade paperback edition published 2003

Book design by Jessica Shatan

The Library of Congress has cataloged the hardcover edition as follows:
Guthrie, Elisabeth.
The trouble with perfect: How to find success and balance in a hyper-competitive world / Elisabeth Guthrie and
Kathy Matthews.—1st ed.
p. cm.
1. Child rearing. 2. Parenting. 3. Parent and child. I. Matthews, Kathy.
II. Title.
HQ769.G954 2001
649'.1—dc21
2001043403

ISBN 0-7679-0752-3

1   3   5   7   9   10   8   6   4   2

To the children, families, staff, and supporters
of Blythedale Children's Hospital

ACKNOWLEDGMENTS

I would like to express my sincere gratitude to Kathy Matthews for the diligence, skill, and sense of humor she brought to this project. I thank our agent Laureen Rowland for her savvy and steadfast support. I also wish to thank Trish Medved, our editor, and James Benson, her assistant, for their availability and expertise. Thank you also to Gerry Howard, Steve Rubin, and Michael Palgon of Broadway Books. I am indebted to my patients, their families, and my colleagues for the opportunity to work with them. I would like to thank Dr. Sidney Carter, who led me to Blythedale Children's Hospital, and my coworkers, particularly those in the Department of Psychiatry/Psychology, as well as Mr. Stone, who helped to keep me there. A special thank-you to the memory of Dr. Norman Roberts. I am also grateful to Donna Zanolla, Judy Patsalos, Judy Brazen, Emily

Brichetta, Robin Zucker, Larry Levine, Ellen Slansky, Jill Linder, Jane Brody, Connie Cornell, Madeline Ginzberg, and Betty Hart for their wisdom and encouragement. And of course, I wish to acknowledge my family for their patience and understanding.

—EG

I am grateful to Dr. Guthrie, who made *No More Push Parenting* an exhilarating and unforgettable experience. Laureen Rowland was everything that one could hope for in an agent as well as a friend and unwavering supporter. Trish Medved at Broadway Books was enthusiastic and hardworking throughout the editorial process as was her assistant, James Benson. Gerry Howard of Broadway Books was an early supporter of this book, and I'm grateful to him as well as his colleagues Steve Rubin and Michael Palgon. Friends who have been particularly helpful in sharing experiences and ideas include Diane Essig, Maggie Peterson, Julie Houston, Jean Drumm, Julie Karpeh, Nancy Nolan, and Markie Robson-Scott. I am in their debt.

—KM

CONTENTS

The World of Almost Perfect

Josh and Max are eleven-year-old twins. Twice a week they are awakened at four-thirty in the morning, dressed in the dark, and driven to hockey practice. They eat Pop Tarts en route. Their father is very enthusiastic about the boys' hockey—he calls them his double threat—and he's gotten them expensive gear bags and new sticks for their birthday. The boys' mother is ambivalent. Josh and Max both have fallen asleep at their desks at school in the past weeks. But, shrugging, she claims, "They just love it. And their dad is so proud of them."

Ginny is a sophomore at a prestigious private school in New York. Her older brother attends an Ivy League college, their father's alma mater. Ginny is getting C's and B's in school, and her highly successful parents call me, worried. Even though they've had no other physician referral and no teacher complaints or concerns, they wonder if it's possible that Ginny has Attention Deficit Hyperactivity Disorder. Perhaps, her mother suggests, she should be on medication.

Maya, a shy and anxious fourteen-year-old, sits in my office and talks about how annoyed her mother must be with her. Last week, on the way to the hospital, Maya cried and begged her mother to cancel the nose job that they had scheduled for her as a birthday present. Maya had originally agreed to the surgery, knowing it would please her mother, but she had never really wanted it. Mother, who was driving, and Grandma, who was along for moral support, finally gave in and brought her home.

It used to be that there were three kinds of children: average, above average, and below average. And while all but the most popular kids were sometimes teased for being chosen last for the team, or for being short (or tall), or thin (or fat), or for being dumb (or smart), most of us managed to survive. We got B's, some C's, and occasionally A's. We had a few close friends and a bunch of hallway pals. We had a few interests, maybe played a sport. We hung out a lot. And while our parents complained about the usual, like our messy rooms, they pretty much left us alone.

Of course, there was always one kid in the class who seemed to be born with an oboe in his mouth, and who knew from the age of five that he "always wanted to attend Harvard and become a neurologist." Indeed, while we were average or above average, healthy and well-adjusted, that kid was just plain *weird.*

Today, it seems many parents yearn to have the kind of perfect child we would have once considered weird—overly ambitious, hypercompetitive, serious to a fault—and are doing everything within their power to craft one. We meet kids like Josh, Max, Ginny, and Maya every single day. Good, hard-working, above-average kids whose parents are constantly "encouraging" them to take violin lessons (with the best teacher in the state) and to prepare for the SATs (with a tutor) as early as the ninth grade. These are the parents who are pushing their animal-loving daughter to consider a pre-med major just "because you're guaranteed six figures as a doctor."

To these parents, B's aren't good enough, nor is simply getting into a good college. It's got to be Ivy League, or it may as well be nothing. Playing a single sport isn't good enough. It's got to be soccer in the fall, basketball in the winter, track in the spring (and it's important to be a captain of at least one of these teams). To these parents—a great many of the parents in our society today—what was once considered above average has become average. And what was once considered so significant to a child's development—the freedom to identify and pursue one's own individual talents and interests—has been replaced by that which will appear most impressive to the outside world. The elusive goal for these children is perfection.

We have become so accustomed to hearing about these kinds of excesses in parenting—about overscheduled toddlers, pressured children, and superachieving teens—that we have really, to some degree, lost our sense of perspective. We shrug, and think of the neighbor or PTA acquaintance who's done the same or worse, and move on. But the fact is, we *don't* really move on. More and more we're affected, as parents, with tremendous anxiety and a constant low drumbeat of pressure from the questions we ask ourselves again and again: Are we doing enough for our kids? Should we be doing more? Will our kids measure up?

Certainly the parents of the children described in the above scenarios are basically reasonable and sensible. Probably people like you and me. I know from many conversations with such parents that most of them, like Josh and Max's mom, wonder if all the pressure they are putting on their children is ultimately bad. After all, their own parents paid little attention to the details of their upbringing, and they're doing fine today.

THE PRICE OF PERFECT

Most parents smile with recognition or nod knowingly when I mention the term "push parenting." They see it all around them. It's evident in behaviors like:

- Orchestrating virtually every moment of a child's life with lessons, play dates, and "enriching activities";

- Demanding high achievement in school and at sports at almost any cost (emotional, psychological, physiological, financial);

- Pressuring a child to choose courses, activities, or interests more to "build a résumé" than to discover or explore natural curiosities or personal interests;

- Meddling in a child's friendships and relations with teachers and coaches.

There is, of course, a fine line between effective, responsible parenting and "push parenting." Most of us do not fall prey to the extreme of insisting that a child be unjustifiably labeled as "learning disabled" so she will have extra time to take tests; coaching Little League only so we can put our child in every game and send him to the state "all-star" playoffs; or attempting to influence the admissions officer of our child's first-choice college with a large "contribution." Certainly, some do. But the phenomenon of push parenting is less about these somewhat isolated extremes and more about the messages we are sending our children on a daily basis when we push: That they are not capable of making responsible choices by themselves. That appearances are more important than authenticity. That it is less important for them to own their experiences than it is to hold a socially significant title (track star, honor student, Harvard grad).

That we don't trust them to succeed without our help.

This book is an effort to help parents understand what motivates them to lose confidence in their child's ability to succeed independently. Most of us are motivated by the best of intentions: We want what is best for our children. But many of us find ourselves being pushed off track by cultural pressures, and we're only dimly aware that it's happening. I think it's both reassuring and enlightening to explore the forces that shape us as parents in today's world.

WHY DO WE PUSH?

Consider the following situations and, if you are a parent, it will be hard to silence the buzz of anxiety in the back of your mind:

The local paper reports that Barbara G., your daughter's classmate, has just been accepted, early decision, at Harvard. About to graduate first in her class, she is captain of the softball and basketball teams, and her pastels have been featured in a state exhibition of talented high school artists. She's stud-

ied art in Japan and France on summer vacations. Your daughter is still "thinking" about her college application essays and angrily rejects your help.

It seems that every child in your town plays baseball, except yours. He has zero interest in organized sports and has told you that if you sign him up for baseball, he won't go. The other kids seem to be learning skills and making friends while your child is missing out.

The fifth-grade awards assembly is over. It was a generous program, with many categories and many winners. Your son is one of the handful of students who did not receive any awards at all. You are searching for something to say to him as you buckle up for the drive home, which suddenly seems very long.

Your nine-year-old daughter has decided that she is not going to continue with her piano lessons, and nothing you can do will change her mind. She's sick of practicing and she never wants to play again. You've been paying for lessons for two years now, and you don't think it's really important to play, but she has no other extracurricular activities or special interests, and that concerns you.

Your friend just told you that her daughter is on the waiting list for the best SAT prep course in your area. Her daughter is in eighth grade. So is yours. The SATs are three years away. You get that old familiar sinking feeling. Should you sign your daughter up, too?

How do many otherwise sensible and reasonable parents react to these "B+" situations? They start to think about what it takes to get to "A." They start to think about what they could do to get their child to "A." They start to feel the pressure to improve their "almost perfect" child.

The pressure to push is pervasive. Writers and editors in the mainstream press, undoubtedly struggling with this issue with their own children, have responded to the subject with an on-slaught of articles. *The Wall Street Journal* has featured pieces on which sports most appeal to Ivy League recruiters; the *New York Observer* has compiled a guide to the most effective/expensive SAT tutors. *New York* magazine recently featured a cover story entitled "What Your Four-Year-Old Doesn't Know Could Ruin His Life."

Information that used to be available in the school board's office to the rare parent who sought it out—on how the local school rates in the district and the region—is now headline news in local papers and national news magazines. *Newsweek* recently rated national high schools based on what many would consider a flimsy scale having to do with the percentage of students taking advanced courses and passing the exams for them.

There is also the vast and burgeoning achievement industry of tutors, coaches, and educational games that sells "cognitive enhancement" in the form of learning toys, study guides, and SAT prep books. And, thanks to the bull market of the nineties, many parents have the wherewithal to respond feverishly, enabling them to indulge every self-improvement fantasy in giving their children "opportunities" (advantages) that they themselves didn't have. For many parents today, no tutor or sports equipment is too expensive—it is, after all, a "worthwhile investment."

It's not only academic or athletic achievement that falls into the "must improve" category, either. Amazingly, even a child's physical appearance is now seen as something to be evaluated rather than accepted. A large nose or a fanny that's a bit too am-ple to look good in Capri pants can be altered relatively easily, if not with makeup and diet, then through surgery or liposuction. While beauty used to be skin deep, now it's only as deep as your pocket, which, for many parents these days, is rather deep indeed.

Finally, there's the social "justification" for parents to leap onto the "pressure" bandwagon: Sound bites of scientific research on child development have been oversimplified in the popular press to the point where parents have come to believe that black-and-white mobiles and French tapes for toddlers really will give their child the significant boost they need to be successful. The emphasis is no longer on whether the child might discover a facility with another language at a young age and so open a window of discovery and experience. Rather, the emphasis has shifted to such an extent that parents today have come to feel that they are inadequate or even negligent if they aren't booking their little one for Gymboree classes and filling the playpen with stimulating toys from Zainy Brainy.

But perhaps the most compelling issue for parents who can't resist the urge to push is fear. Parents want their children to be happy. They equate success with happiness, and feel a tremendous responsibility to arm their children with the necessary tools to succeed. In a hypercompetitive world, we push because we care.

THE TROUBLE WITH PERFECT

What's a parent to do? I have had conversations with countless mothers and fathers who are concerned about the parenting culture they see all around them. They don't want to get sucked in, but they don't know how not to. They feel too much is at stake. This book does not try to tell you how to stop push parenting, how to change the culture, or how to reinvent your family. What I've tried to do is outline some of the pressures and motives that fuel the competitive parenting that is so dismaying to so many of us. I've tried to point out some of the consequences of push parenting and what can happen to you, your child, and your family when you allow the focus to shift from enjoying your child and helping him or her mature to building your child's résumé as a bridge to the future. I believe that when parents reevaluate their goals for themselves and their children in a fresh light, they'll be relieved to realize that their best instincts are probably the best guide to parenting in today's world.

PART I

Resisting the Hypes That Make You Push

Introducing the Seven Hypes

When did you first feel it? Was it when your son was the last in his play group to learn to speak? When your daughter's pre-school interview was a screaming-dervish tantrum disaster? When your son's batting in T-ball was right out of Monty Python? When your middle-schooler wasn't recommended for a single honors class?

We all face it at some point: the realization that our children, at least in some respects, aren't the best, brightest, prettiest, fastest, most enviable and perfect specimens who ever walked the earth. It can be a devastating feeling. One minute you are living the fantasy—beaming as your child accepts the Heisman Trophy, Nobel Peace Prize, or National Book Award—and the next you are sitting in the dust with this rather, well, ordinary child.

For most of us as parents, these moments of recognizing our child's frailties are an opportunity for growth: Ideally, we empathize with our child and create an appropriate strategy for dealing with the situation. In many cases, the only strategy is acceptance and love. Maybe our son won't be the Sammy Sosa of Westchester. Maybe our daughter will be better off in another nursery school. Sometimes, a bit of help is in order. A check with the pediatrician can confirm that a nonspeaking toddler doesn't have a hearing problem that's affecting speech. A check with the guidance counselor at school may reassure you about your son's nonhonors status, or encourage you to follow procedures for him to try an honors course on a trial basis.

But wait a minute . . . Are you thinking that isn't the kind of help you had in mind? Are you thinking that you know a top-notch coach for that T-baller? Are you thinking that a letter from your neighbor, a heavy-hitting fund-raiser at the nursery school, could make the difference with the headmaster and convince her your daughter doesn't always act like she needs an exorcism? Perhaps you're thinking that a few calls to teachers, promises of tutors, and maybe even taking on a serious PTA job could convince that middle-school principal to be a little more liberal with his honors-class placements?

As we try to sort out what strategy makes sense—the coach or maybe a bit of backyard practice; the donation or maybe a more low-key nursery school—we can't avoid the stress of these decisions. Actually the stress of parenting is made up of these kinds of decisions, and they become more complicated as our lives become more demanding and our culture becomes more competitive. It's very hard to sort out what's a sensible choice when we're feeling the impulse to push our children.

As Mel Levine, a highly esteemed developmental pediatrician, says, "Adults can be specialists; children must be generalists." We can decide we're good at teaching and not tennis, or good at financial research and not cleaning. We make our life choices based on these proclivities and skills, and, with luck and determination, we find roles that suit us and make us happy. But our kids have to be good at math, English, science, sports, community service, leadership, foreign languages, and so on. As the bar has been raised for them, the stress and pressure to perform becomes more and more intense. Unfortunately, a large part of this stress and pressure is due to the demands we, as parents, make on them. We want our kids to do well and get ahead. This is reasonable and important. But we don't want to push them so hard that the results are negative. Indeed, this is the theme of this book: How do you encourage your child to achieve in a healthy way? How do you judge how much nudging is good and how much is counterproductive?

Some parents don't care: They're going to push no matter what. Parents of this sort are not reflective or introspective. It's very difficult to get them to change course or even consider reassessing their goals. But you, if you are reading this book, are probably different. You're open to change. You're worried about achieving the right balance in your child's life. You're willing to ask the right questions. I've seen many parents like you, too; parents who are concerned about the stressful world their children are entering and how they can help them achieve without destroying the spark that makes them unique.

Unfortunately, many of today's parents, many of *us,* go at this whole parenting thing full tilt. For reasons, some good and some misguided, that we'll explore, we feel that our child's ultimate success is all up to us, and that the goal is to win, or to get our kids to win. This is not news to you. You've read the articles about test prepping for the best colleges that rivals astronaut training; bar mitzvahs that demand the financial and emotional fortitude of a Broadway producer; and athletic competition so fierce that it has actually been fatal to at least one parent.

Why *are* we so competitive when it comes to our children? Why are we convinced that it's so important for them to have a dazzling résumé? To have a "passion"? To stand out, in some way, from the crowd? What is it that makes intelligent, sensible parents prep their young child for an IQ test, or hire a sixty-dollar-an-hour coach for their beginning Little Leaguer, or drive a half hour after a busy workday to bring a toddler to an art class when everybody might be happier at home enjoying dinner or bath time?

What I have learned from countless parents is that just about no one wants to push, but most feel they must. They've come to believe in a fearful and anxious way that they as parents or, more crucially, their children will fall short in the relentless competition of everyday life if they don't keep pushing.

The great, gnawing fear is that if you don't push, if you relax and let the chips fall where they may, your child will fail. Or at least not succeed. That's the fear-inducing truth that most of us wrestle with when we try to decide if we should call the teacher and challenge a grade, if we should sign our child up for SAT coaching starting in eighth grade, if we should encourage our child to try out for the crew team because we've heard that Ivy League schools are high on rowing.

But is it true? Is it true that our children need us to give them that extra edge? Is it possible that it can be counterproductive to do so?

As parents, we're used to following our impulse: When the baby cries, we tend to her. When the toddler falls, we comfort him. To some degree, we must rely on our impulses to guide us in our child-rearing. And if our impulse to push, prod, and maneuver our child is so strong that it almost becomes an imperative, then perhaps it's an impulse that should be obeyed.

But most of us *do* have a little voice inside that says, "This is crazy; this is too much."

First, of course, we must acknowledge that people are naturally competitive. There are basic human impulses that make us want to be the best, make us want our children to be the best. In the version of the jungle that most of us inhabit, the richest man gets the prettiest girl (and the biggest house, the most luxurious car, and the most frequent-flyer miles). But, fortunately, we all have minds and souls and are able to conceptualize a vast panoply of satisfactions that life has to offer beyond a babe, a stretch, and five thousand square feet of living space.

Sad to say, despite our higher reasoning abilities, some notions endure—many just vague, unrecognized concepts in the back of our minds—that direct our behavior as parents. These notions—or "hypes"—are usually unexamined and even unrecognized, but they can cloud our decisions and encourage us to act in ways that are irrational, yes, but more important, damaging to our children. At first glance, these hypes seem like a monolithic force: difficult to assess, impossible to resist. But I think you can separate out individual cultural pressures, and it's helpful to do so. What follows is an exploration of seven hypes that I see parents struggling with daily and some ideas on how you can resist them to bring more balance into your life with your child.

Everybody's Doing It!

If there could be a Unilateral Push-Parenting Disarmament Treaty, we'd all stop, but as it is, if we relax, let up, cancel the tutor, our kid will miss out, fall behind, fail.

The culture makes us push.

We hear it in the ob/gyn waiting room, on the sidelines of the soccer field, during the coffee break at the PTA meeting, in line at the grocery store . . . "If you don't hold the baby skin-to-skin immediately after birth, you'll compromise bonding." "If they don't begin a language by age three, it will be much harder for them to learn when they're older." "If they don't do T-ball, they'll never be able to play baseball because the other kids will be so far ahead of them." "If they don't get into honors math in eighth grade, they'll never get into calculus in high school." "If they don't start working on their ECs (that's "extracurriculars" to the uninitiated) in middle school, it doesn't look good because colleges like to see consistency and long-term commitment."

We live in a land of opportunity, a democracy that promises equal access for all. To the founding fathers, this meant no man would be denied freedoms on the basis of his religion. To a mother in the twenty-first century, it means that all the strollers are lined up at the starting line, and it's every baby for him- or herself. (Of course, mom pushes and steers for the first eighteen years.)

With the advent of fertility issues, the pressure to succeed begins before conception. I recently saw a brief segment of a show on Lifetime TV that featured an alarmingly solemn young couple recounting "their pregnancy experience." They had been advised to adopt a macrobiotic diet to "cleanse" their bodies and prepare for the most optimum time of conception. After four months of this diet, they were advised by their counselor that they could "begin trying." As expected, they conceived immediately. They seemed to believe that they had gotten a very fast out-of-the-gate start for their baby. They had every intention of maintaining this lead by restricting themselves to a strict organic, macrobiotic diet for the duration of the pregnancy.

It seems that no decision regarding the gestation or birth of a middle-class baby in this country can be taken lightly. No one comparison-shops like a woman pregnant with her first child. Cloth or Pampers? Epidural or natural childbirth? Episiotomy or prayer? Perego or Maclaren?

This is the beginning of the real sense that a pregnant woman feels that she is responsible for the ultimate health, intelligence, and, indeed, the very success of her child. Because the implication is that by doing or avoiding certain things she will create a better baby. She'll never have to look back and say, "If it weren't for those daily milligrams of caffeine, perhaps she would have been a National Merit Scholar," or "If only I'd eaten more carrots, his vision would be better, and he'd have been accepted to the Air Force flight training school," or "If only I'd breastfed for a year instead of a paltry two months, maybe she wouldn't have that allergy."

The guilt that women feel today over less than "perfect" births is truly overwhelming because they've been led to believe that if they just had had the discipline and education to make the right choices, nothing would ever go wrong. An educated and sophisticated woman I know was devastated after the birth of her first child. She had done everything right. But her labor didn't progress and she'd ultimately had a C-section. As she said, "I was so disappointed that I couldn't really enjoy the baby. I spent the first few weeks of his life reviewing the labor over and over, and wondering if there was anything I could have done differently, anything I could have done in advance, that would have resulted in a natural childbirth."

Of course, as any neonatal nurse or obstetrician or labor coach can tell you, things happen. Even when it comes to the most disciplined, educated, determined mothers, despite the fact that better prenatal care has resulted in healthier babies and fewer risky births, there is an inevitable percentage of birth problems, low Apgar scores, and less than perfect babies. Unfortunately, the real-life fact of simple bad luck is often obscured by the hype. By the time your baby enters the world in today's culture, you've already been thoroughly inculcated to understand and accept that whatever happens to this child, this little Rembrandt or Mozart or Doug Flutie, it will be due in large part to your efforts.

At least in utero, it's just you and your fetus. It's not so hard to control what you eat and drink and listen to. And there's still the mystery of this little creature to be. But right after delivery you're assaulted with the outside world. The baby is big or small or alert or sleepy or more or less hungry than your neighbor's. That's when you begin to realize that a barely audible gun has gone off and the starting flag is waving.

You want what is best for your baby. As a new parent you're just trying to figure out what the heck that is. One thing's for sure: You're not certain of anything anymore. And you're extremely vulnerable to suggestions, criticisms, and "expert" advice. You're looking for answers. And this is what you see:

Your neighbors push, your sister-in-law pushes, every parent on every TV show pushes, whether it's with a three-year-old who's learning Japanese or a Halloween costume that looks like it came from a production of *The Lion King*. Don Imus, the morning radio host who plays political conscience to the cappuccino crowd, discusses his two-year-old's Spanish lessons on air. The media barrage us relentlessly with stories of super-achieving kids and how they got that way. The *Today* show recently featured a two-year-old with an extraordinary golf swing and, a few segments later, a woman touted her new book outlining how your infant's IQ could be increased by certain physical exercises.

Eventually your cheerful little mud-pie maker, TV watcher, videogamer begins to seem somewhat lackluster. Not that we think any the less of our children in comparison to the spectacular children we see all around. But we begin to worry that the world won't see how great they are, how special. That they won't reap the rewards that other children reap, that they won't measure up in the world's view.

We feel the little tingle of envy and competition, even when we know that what we are watching or reading is baloney. For instance, a popular women's magazine recently featured a story on child actors. Six attractive and successful children from age 8 through age 15 were profiled. Aside from their acting, money, friendships with stars, busy travel schedules, and so forth, they were purported to be "just like any other kid." According to their proud moms, they all had friends, chores, homework, and pet peeves. They're sort of super-average. Just a tick above our own child in skills, ability, determination. Why, we begin to think, can't my own little one have a starring role in a major motion picture? What would I have to do to get that going? We allow ourselves to feel this way, even though we have, last month in that same magazine, read an article about the drug re-habs, the family estrangements, the teen divorces, and the real misery that the lives of a half-dozen child actors have become.

Of course, few of us will make any move toward encouraging our child's acting career. But it's something else entirely when we grapple with the nexus of competition that daily life with children throws us into, whether we're discussing when they first slept through the night, what good eaters they are, when the training wheels came off their bikes, or if they made the all-star travel team, and what their SAT scores were.

When we're faced with these small, inevitable hot spots of competition, we want our child to be just a smidge better than the kid next door. Or at least as good as the kid next door. So if the neighbor's kid is being tutored in math, privately coached for T-ball, prepped for nursery school interviews, then we feel the pressure to do the same. After all, we're all looking for that elusive "level playing field."

Many of us who are parents now believe we experienced this level playing field for one brief shining moment when we took the SATs years ago. (We were unaware that socioeconomics and gender greatly impacted where our scores fell.) In those days, no one really "prepared" for the test. We were told you couldn't really prepare and we believed it. We simply walked in with our number-two pencils and took it. In a perfect world, we think, our own children would be able to walk into an SAT test unprepared. But if they do, they'll be in a distinct minority. SAT-test prep has become an industry. There are books, CDs, Web sites, courses, and tutors all geared to helping your child lift a score by a few or many points. It truly seems that if you don't encourage your child to prep for the SAT, it practically qualifies as middle-class child neglect.

Many parents use this "fact"—their own history with the SATs—to extrapolate to other tutoring and "extra-credit" parenting efforts. The reasoning is that once upon a time parents could ignore all this and their kids would be fine. But times have changed. Today everybody is prepping their child, and what used to be an extra is now a requirement

While most parents are somewhat disgusted the first time someone asks where their infant is going to nursery school, they soon begin to realize that they really do have to begin thinking ahead. Because the good nursery school in town has a waiting list. And if you don't get in for the "Just for Twos" program, you'll probably be squeezed out of the "Blue Room" when your child turns three, and then the "Red Room" will be home to only those four-year-olds whose parents were smart right from the beginning. If everyone else stopped and lived in the moment, of course you could, too. But how can you relax when everyone else is thinking ten steps ahead?

It's like campaign finance reform: Everyone agrees that it's a great idea, but no one wants to be the first to limit their war chest.

The notion that there's not enough success to go around feeds the frenzy of competitive parenting. This notion is, in turn, based on the idea that there are only so many places at the best schools—nursery, prep, and college—and if you don't get one of the slots, all is lost. If success, like the number of available PT Cruisers or top-notch music teachers, is limited, then we're right to be worried.

Consider musical chairs. Your toddler is at a birthday party, and the chairs are arranged in a circle. Nine children in a barely controlled frenzy circle around eight chairs. Suddenly the music stops. Bodies fly, chairs are grabbed, and when the dust settles, your little one is left, the only one standing. It's difficult to know who is more devastated; only half a lifetime of socialization keeps you from dashing into the next room and finding yet another chair.

Musical chairs is a very simple game. The winners sit and the loser stands. There are no gray areas. And there is no chance to modify the game: You can't share a chair with your best friend. You can't gain points by running faster or slower. You can't get someone's chair by putting up a dazzling argument. In each round, one person is eliminated. In the end, one person wins. There is a very limited amount of available success.

Many parents today view their life with their children as a very important game of musical chairs. But instead of the ultimate goal being to find a seat, the ultimate goal is to find "success." And the most significant part of this analogy is the view that *there is a limited amount of success.* If your child gets a chair, mine might not. If my child moves sluggishly, isn't alert enough, isn't in the right place at the right time, he will have failed because someone else will grab his place.

The collateral notion is that every other child, every one competing with my child, is the enemy. Or at least the competition.

Is this realistic? Is this how life works? Well, many adults can correctly answer that, yes, this is how their life works. They got a promotion and a raise while someone else lost out. They got the last tickets because they outsmarted the hordes and called in a favor from a booking agent. They got their great apartment because they befriended the doorman. In other words, they figured things out in advance, went the extra mile, and won. So, yes, for adults, viewing many aspects of life as a competition is accurate and perhaps even useful. But is it an appropriate and useful model to use in guiding *children* and in making decisions about their lives?

Most parents have come to accept the "school" model of life. As acceptance at a very selective school (nursery school, prep school, college) becomes an ultimate goal, the notion of "limited success" determines children's lives. If there are only five or fifty or one hundred open slots, how can we arrange for our child to have one of them? This is a fast-paced, high-stakes game of musical chairs, and only the best will win.

But all the evidence to the contrary is ignored. The business tycoon, like Bill Gates, who dropped out of college. The impressive success of Charles Schwab, founder of the famous investment firm, who suffered from learning disabilities.

Certainly there's a constant barrage of information to keep you as a parent feeling frantic.

SAT fever has now trickled down to nursery school prep. A recent article in the *New York Times* discussed consultants in New York who charge up to three hundred dollars an hour to guide parents through the nursery and elementary school application process. One consultant charges six hundred dollars for nursery school applications and fifteen hundred dollars for elementary school applications including two ninety-minute consultations. Children are taught to make eye contact, smile, and share. And then, if they are old enough, they are taught to be natural, so no one will suspect that they've been prepped.

There's great secrecy about this grooming because, as you might imagine, the schools strongly discourage it. Why would anyone pay this kind of money to "prep" a three- to five-year-old for something that they're not supposed to be prepped for in the first place? As Mark H. Sklarow, the executive director of the Independent Educational Consultants Association, a professional association based in Virginia, puts it in the *New York Times:* "Parents generally have a very skewed perception of the private school world. They're convinced that if they don't get into a good nursery school, they're never going to get into the right prep school, they won't get into Harvard, and their life is over."

It's the rather extreme end of the anxiety scale that is focused on getting "only the best" for a child. Of course, reading and hearing about it only make it worse for those fence-sitters who never even considered such a thing, but now wonder if perhaps their child will be at a disadvantage if he just wanders in off the street, head filled with superheroes and pizza, for an interview that might change his life.

As the student population grows and the business of "improving" children via tutors and coaches becomes heavily invested in preserving parental anxiety, the pressure to excel creates a crush of competition that takes on a life of its own. In a recent article in the *Hartford Courant,* it was reported that six years ago, half of the eighth-grade class at the Independent Day School in Middlefield, Connecticut, was admitted to Choate Rosemary Hall, an exclusive college preparatory school. This year, only a handful were admitted. Peter Philip, the dean of admissions at Hotchkiss, reports that applications to his school are up a third since 1995. The admission rate is running at 27 percent.

The mother of a sixth-grade applicant to a New York City private school advised in a local paper, "It was really important this year to get started in early September. Some people waited too long and are now at a disadvantage. You have to get going early and move with vigor, so that testing, tours, tutoring, and interviews are completed by the middle of December." Whew!

In the spring of 2001 National Public Radio invited high school seniors to submit their college application essays to the network. Out of the 150 sent by students, parents, guidance counselors, and friends, five were selected to be read on the air. Many college applications ask for a heartfelt discussion of something that a student feels has deeply affected his or her life. One of the essays, for example, discussed the student's battle with anorexia. While it is certainly interesting to hear how high school seniors are handling the challenge of selling themselves to a college in their application essays, it's a corruption of the process to broadcast the results. These essays were not written to be published, or even to be shared with anyone other than the admissions committee. Not only does the broadcasting of the student's essays seem to tarnish the process, it also serves to ratchet up the level of competition that other parents and students already feel. It emphasizes the gamesmanship involved, while at the same time devaluing the purpose of the essay itself.

These reports and countless others flood the media, driving up parental anxiety to almost unbearable levels. The message is quite clear. If you want your child to succeed, don't wait another minute: Get him on the team, get her tutored, get your ducks in a row because time's a-wasting.

There is nothing wrong with these feelings of competitiveness and the resulting anxiety; indeed, they are absolutely normal. A large part of our parental mission is to launch our child into the world as well equipped as possible to survive and, we hope, succeed. The trouble can develop when we take our cues from current parenting culture rather than from our child. For many parents and their children the race, toward Harvard, Princeton, or their near equivalent, begins early and becomes the informing spirit behind many parenting decisions.

This intense focus on feverish improvement and performance, fueled by the media, the economy, and the neighbors, obscures some important truths about children and growth and development. It is one thing for a sixteen-year-old to take a test prep course that will help him gain confidence and perhaps refresh him on a few math formulas; it is quite another to create an atmosphere where a child, from the age of two, feels the constant pressure to improve, to become something "better," or perhaps "other," than he or she really is.

One of the scourges of contemporary parenting that seems to play into the "everybody's doing it" compulsion is the relentless focus on goals. Parents feel that because they can "do it all," so can their children. Parents exist in goal-oriented settings. We're all expected to meet certain goals at work. Even some of our leisure is goal-oriented: We ride a bike to raise our heartbeat to a target range and improve our health. We take courses to improve ourselves. We've learned to enjoy the results of our efforts. It's satisfying to lose weight or learn a new language. Of course, it's easy to project these feelings onto our children. Won't they feel great when they make the team, win the math competition, learn to play that piano piece? Well, achievement does feel good to anyone, but for children, it's the process that counts. And achievement feels best when it's a goal you've set for yourself, not one that's been imposed on you.

The story of Bill Johnson, the gifted downhill skiing champion who brought home Olympic gold from Sarajevo, Yugoslavia, in 1984, provides a tragic perspective on living for a goal. No one is more obsessively goal-oriented than an athlete, and no doubt success at the highest levels of sport demands total dedication. (As Lynn Jennings, winner of six U.S. titles in outdoor track, says, "If I'm not out there training, someone else is.") Bill Johnson was determined to make it to the 2002 Olympics after his triumph in the eighties, but, as an older skier at age 40, he faced tremendous odds. Fighting to get the attention of American coaches, he was almost killed as he lost his balance and crashed on a dangerous curve at the U.S. Alpine Championships. Sadly, Johnson's life after his initial Olympic triumph had unraveled. He was divorced from his wife, away from his two young sons, and without a job, or even a permanent residence. As one of his longtime friends told the *New York Times,* "When Billy was a kid, his vision was to win the gold medal. I don't think he ever knew what the next vision for him was. The sad part is that Billy has struggled the whole rest of his life with the next vision."

An unbalanced focus on the goal or prize, particularly when the quest involves children, can be counterproductive. One mother made an interesting point when discussing with me her sense that she had pushed her now-grown children. "I always told them to do your best, be your best. But I now think that maybe they thought I was telling them they must always win." This mom's perception was right: To a child, "your best" can mean *perfect.* Few children feel they can achieve perfection. And if they try to, the fear of failing can create tremendous stress.

We feel justified as a generation in pushing our children to succeed because we can see firsthand the results of hard work and the rewards of skillful navigation through life's challenges. Most of us got through college, found a career, make sufficient money, and live comfortable lives. We know what it took to do that. Many of us have more than our parents had, and we want our children to have at least as much as we do. Looking back at our trajectory through life, it's easy to see how we made the right moves (or misstepped sometimes). We know what we're talking about when we tell our children that it's better to take Latin or physics or take up fencing instead of hockey.

What we forget is that we have made a seismic shift—one we're generally unaware of—in what we expect of children and the stresses we create in their lives. We have gone from a child-centered culture to a parent-centered one. As David Elkind points out in *The Postmodern Family: A New Imbalance,* parents have changed their attitudes about children to fit the new demands of adult life. "We used to view children as innocent," he says. "Now we think of them as competent. In the same way we used to see teenagers as basically immature, and now we view them as sophisticated. We need to see them that way because we need to feel that they can deal with the modern world." If we need to leave our children alone, in day care, or with a sitter because we're working, we need to feel our children are competent to handle this. If our children need to be home alone after school for a few hours before we get home from work, we need to believe this won't be a problem. If we need to send them alone on a plane to visit an ex-spouse, we can't afford to think they're too young to handle the experience. Over time, we've come to believe that children are closer to small adults than anyone fifty years ago would have believed. This conviction allows us to demand things of them in terms of behavior and achievement that are really beyond the realm of childhood. We're bolstered in our belief that this is appropriate because "everybody's doing it."

It's extremely difficult as a parent to step back and stem the tide. We feel, to modify Lynn Jennings, that if we're not out there parenting, somebody else is. Fortunately, some parents are beginning to move toward a de-escalation of parent fever. An organization called Family Life 1st!, based in an affluent Minneapolis suburb, recently attracted press notice when it asked athletic coaches to cut back on required games and practices, especially during holidays and vacations. Some coaches and parents objected: They see athletics as a wonderful, healthy outlet for their children, to say nothing of a great entrée into a pool of college applicants that can boast "athlete" as well as "scholar" credentials. But many other parents embraced the notion that it was time to cut back on the dominance of activities that take the focus away from the family and allow children some downtime to just be children.

Nine Out of Ten Experts Say So!

We push our children because "experts" have told us that it works. They've recommended optimum prenatal diets, baby brain stimulators, toddler enrichment programs, and the best, least damaging, way to say "no." Despite the fact that we've all grown up without such enhancements, we've come to believe that if we don't make the most of every developmental opportunity, beginning at conception, our children will fall behind.

We Americans are nothing if not new and improved. Sometimes it seems that the guiding principle of our lives is that we must get or be better. Most of us regularly feel the virtuous urge to join a health club, take a course, be a better friend, or get a better job. Unfortunately, many of us expect the same of our children—and we expect the road to improvement to begin in utero.

Thank goodness we all do have the urge to improve. It gets us up in the morning and keeps us, or most of us, from eating all our children's Halloween candy. Most of us could use some improvement. We are presumably mature and capable of making intellectual decisions about our goals in life and the price we will pay to achieve those goals. We know that giving up a daily chocolate may be painful, but the sacrifice could have a satisfying result: zipping up those stretch jeans. Babies, particularly embryos, are another story.

The truth is that much of what we believe when it comes to brain development and our ability to give our children superior mental powers is based on faulty or misguided conclusions from questionable research.

Once upon a time, when our parents were raising us, the general belief was that your genes determined how smart or dumb you were. In *How the Mind Works,* a book by C. Burt and others, published in 1934, the case was simply put: "By intelligence, the psychologist understands inborn, all-around intellectual ability. It is inherited, or at least innate, not due to teaching or training . . . Fortunately, it can be measured with accuracy and ease." Those were the days! Parents were off the hook. Except for marrying someone with great intellectual/ musical/athletic potential, there wasn't much they could do but stand back and watch their progeny achieve their destiny. What a relief.

Today's parents can only look back and wonder. We live in a world in which every aspect of a baby's development must be attended to, beginning with an optimum diet months before pregnancy begins. Women are encouraged to adopt pre-conception diets that will presumably stimulate the conception of a superior fetus. I once met a pregnant woman who had worked hard for the duration of her pregnancy to avoid any conflict with her husband because she was certain such "negative vibes" would harm her baby. On the one hand, we are fortunate to live in an era when the connection between nutrition and health is firmly established. We are also lucky to know that stress can negatively affect a fetus. On the other hand, no pregnant woman should ever have to be concerned that an occasional argument with a spouse would have any effect, negative or positive, on her baby.

Over the past two decades, some fascinating research has suggested that in utero a fetus can recognize its mother's voice. Some mothers, upon learning of this research and delighted with a specific way to enhance their baby's development, make a concerted effort to "speak" to their embryos in loving and affectionate phrases.

BébéSounds, manufactured by Unisar, appeals to this impulse. A listening and microphone device enables you to "listen, talk, and play music to your unborn baby." "Have a smarter baby," it claims. "Bond with your unborn baby. Increase your child's IQ and speed up your baby's motor development." The implication is that if you can make your baby smarter by talking directly to it, then perhaps you are making it duller by not doing so. It would seem to me that a fetus would benefit as much from overhearing statements like "Would you help me carry this to the car for a dollar?" or "Does this store have a ladies' room?"

It's the extrapolation from knowing a fetus recognizes a mother's voice to deciding that it's an obligation to speak directly to the fetus that can push future moms over the edge.

Or consider music in utero. You've probably heard of the "Mozart Effect," a term coined by French physician Alfred Tomatis. In 1993 a University of Wisconsin–Oshkosh research project "proved," or so it was reported, that listening to music by Mozart aids in the development of cognitive skills, including spatial reasoning. The fact that this study was based on college students, and that its results were later called into question, has done little to change the public's mind: You can make your baby smarter by playing Mozart to it from the time of conception. A few years ago, *Money* magazine reported that Newark Community School for the Arts in New Jersey offered a seventy-dollar music course for babies still languishing in the womb. The dutiful pregnant moms gathered to expose their fetuses to the brain-enhancing strains of Mozart and Vivaldi.

In 1996, Dr. Craig Ramey at the University of Alabama reported to the American Academy for the Advancement of Science that infant stimulation beginning as early as six weeks could increase babies' scores on intelligence tests by fifteen to thirty percent. This was front-page news in the *San Francisco Chronicle.* But if after delivery you're too tired to do the stimulating yourself, you can rely on the "Stim-Mobile" ("an intelligent mobile [as opposed to those dumb ones], it promises to give you a more alert, more content, quieter baby"). The leaflet, "What Can a Baby See?," included with the Stim-Mobile claims "Research indicates that infants given a visually enriched environment are less fussy and are more frequently quiet and attentive when awake than infants who are not given special stimulation . . . Babies given these kinds of stimulation show sustained developmental advantages over infants in less stimulating environments."

If a fetus can be taught to appreciate Mozart, an infant's IQ can be boosted with a mobile, and a toddler can be taught to play violin and speak French, then why not? Wouldn't children who had been given all these gifts be better prepared to live a richer, fuller life? And wouldn't they also, not inconsequentially, be extremely successful as they graduated from the best schools, developed the best résumés, and found the top-paying jobs? Many parents today are living by this dictum: Cram as much as you can into their little skulls and they'll be better and smarter and more successful than all their friends, or at least all of your friends' children. The research is telling us that they're all capable of much, much more, if only we have the patience, time, and dedication to teach them. Of course, we won't know the results for years; our children, as always, are a promise we throw at the future. Wouldn't we be negligent if we didn't at least try?

Given this commonly accepted ethic of the benefits of early exposure, it's interesting to look at the actual results of someone who *has* tried. Nineteen years ago, Glenn Doman created the Evan Thomas Institute, a school intended to make children "intellectually, socially, and physically splendid," according to Doman. Doman, known for his rehabilitative work with brain-injured children and his books such as *How to Teach Your Baby to Read,* is a controversial figure. He believes that his methods of "patterning," which requires children to drill repetitive exercises for up to twelve hours daily "so unused brain cells can be programmed to take over the function of damaged cells," can be adapted for "normal" children who will then, after intensive education, become "splendid." His Better Baby Program encourages parents to prepare baby flash cards for reading, math, and hundreds of facts he calls "bits of intelligence." Parents are instructed to work with their babies, drilling them repetitively until they begin to absorb the Better Baby curriculum.

At the Evan Thomas Institute, just outside Philadelphia, children learn Japanese and study the violin using the Suzuki method. Six- and seven-year-olds study Greek and Latin and read Shakespeare. With a flexible schedule, small class size, and thematic learning for older students, they reap the benefit of what most of us would consider an ideal education.

And do these children go out and conquer the world? Well, not quite. One recent report in *The Wall Street Journal* noted that the eight children who remained at the Evan Thomas

Institute until they graduated at about age 13 had trouble adjusting to the outside world.

Of course, it's not just that such intensive and perhaps misguided force-feeding of "education" doesn't yield results because it ignores social aspects of development. Most of us would strongly suspect that putting children in a hothouse atmosphere would affect their ability to cope with the outside world and limit their ability to enjoy it once they try to rejoin everyday life. But these efforts—to boost a baby's brain power with flash cards, to teach a toddler a foreign language not used in the home—are also based on faulty science. Psychologist Edward Zigler, director of the Yale University Bush Center in Child Development and Social Policy and a founder of Head Start, calls Doman's Better Baby concept "utter and absolute nonsense" and claims that it's based on a "bankrupt theoretical foundation."

While Doman's theories claim to be effective with babies who suffered from brain damage and serious disabilities, the American Academy of Pediatrics has made repeated policy statements insisting that the benefits of this intervention remain unproven. For normal babies, the notion of patterning to stimulate brain development is irrelevant as well as unfounded.

Many parents are greatly confused by the popularity of these baby "improvement" programs because they're unaware of how much the original research may have been distorted. The practical implications of much child development research are seized upon by the press and trumpeted to parents to sell magazines, devices, and books. Most parents don't realize that frequently the original conclusions of research on, for example, fetal brain development are so distorted by the time they reach magazine covers that they are a distant echo of what the original studies attempted to demonstrate or disprove. For instance, many studies that explore the effects of stimulation on infants work with infants in deprived situations. It's certainly true that a neglected infant who is left to his own devices for hours on end will suffer from lack of stimulation. His brain development will probably be delayed. So it's fair to say that certain kinds of auditory and visual stimulation are crucial for infant brain stimulation. Where things go off track is when this news filters down to parents who get the message that they must stimulate their two-month-old's brain. The truth is that, again, for the normal, healthy baby in a normal household, the stimulation of the phone ringing, the toast popping up, the TV going, and the regular interaction with a caregiver is all the stimulation the infant needs or can even use.

Many of Doman's theories, and many other child-rearing theories that have become so popularized today that they are routinely accepted as gospel, are, at best, highly theoretical. This will come as a surprise to those who base at least some of their parenting on the notion of, for example, "critical periods" in a child's development.

The public first became aware of these "critical periods" as a formalized argument in the book *The First Three Years of Life* by Burton L. White. This book made the case for various critical development moments in an infant's life that, once missed, would almost certainly never be entirely made up.

"Bonding" is one of the most popular concepts relying on this "critical periods" notion. Many mothers insist that they must be in skin contact with their newborns for a few hours immediately following birth. This "bonding" is thought to insure a successful emotional relationship with the mother and lay the groundwork for appropriate development in a variety of areas. The truth is that the notion of "bonding" is simply an exaggerated and very formalized symbol of what most normal mothers and infants experience in the course of their early days together immediately after birth. But scientists, looking at the early imprinting of animals like ducklings and goslings, extrapolated this phenomenon to human infants. The two scientists who made these bold claims based their theory on a single study of twenty-eight poor, unmarried women. Despite the flimsy basis for the concept of bonding, most mothers today remain convinced of its validity and feel guilty and anxious if they think that they have missed this critical "bonding," either because of difficulties in delivery or subsequent health problems of the mother or baby or because of adoption.

A cover story in *Time* magazine in 1997 gave impetus to the notion that parents hold the reins to their child's future success. It said that new synapses in the baby's brain are established every time a parent looks down at the infant's face. One child psychologist in the article claimed, "Experiences in the first year of life lay the basis for networks of neurons that enable us to be smart, creative, and adaptable in all the years that follow." This sort of wildly exaggerated claim gives rise to all the mothers you find in supermarkets chatting nonstop with the best of intentions to their sleepy babies, instructing them about everything from the letters in the Alpha-Bits cereal box to where the milk comes from.

Now the pendulum is swinging again. A recent issue of *Time* magazine has a cover story on the new "Superkid," which proclaims in a blurb next to a photo of a four-year-old holding a test tube, "Throw away those flash cards, relax, and let kids be kids. A how-to [and how-not-to] guide for parents." Does this mean we no longer have to chat with our embryos?

Of course, mother and fathers will and should speak to their babies. They should touch them, point things out to them, and let them play with appropriate toys and explore their environment. But they shouldn't do these things because they believe that a smarter, more successful baby will be the result, or if they're motivated by fear that a duller, unsuccessful toddler will result if they don't.

As David Elkind, well-known author of *The Hurried Child*, among other books, points out, the pressure to teach children skills before they are interested or even developmentally ready is, in fact, miseducation. This kind of "miseducation, by focusing upon skills to the detriment of motivation, pays an enormous price for teaching infants and young children what amounts to a few tricks. An ounce of motivation is worth a pound of skills anytime." I have often heard such training referred to among professionals as "stupid baby tricks."

A large body of research demonstrates that children who are exposed to too much early stimulation may be candidates for stress, stomachaches, headaches, eating and sleeping problems, and fragile or low self-esteem. Many research studies also suggest that kindergarten early readers become disillusioned and dispassionate students by age nine, and that adult-stimulated early achievement in young children can result in anxious learners later. Reading too soon, in fact, is often a symptom of developmental pathology, and it is hardly ever the same as reading "on time." Parents are rarely made aware of this research. Certainly it's not front-page news.

As we can see now, so much child-rearing advice gets taken out of context, exaggerated, and twisted beyond recognition that its original proponent may be shocked at what has happened to his recommendation. One example of this sort of distortion involves what I've come to think of as the "P" word: passion. Nowadays it seems that we all want our children to have a "passion." It's obviously wrong to force a child to study, say, astronomy or paleontology. But if the child one night looks up at the stars and asks what they are, or watches a dinosaur documentary and expresses an interest, we as parents feel we've been given the go-ahead. Now it's not us: "It's his passion," and thus we justify the extraordinary lengths to which we can go to foster that "passion." In *The Superbaby Syndrome,* a book published some ten years ago, which is generally a sensible debunking of the myth of the superbaby, the author quotes Ann Jernberg, director of Chicago's Theraplay Institute on ways a parent can help a child learn: "What's important?" asks Jernberg. "Dinner table conversation, books, and magazines," she says, and then veers off into the kind of frenzy that makes for pressured kids and frantic parents. "If your child gets excited about robins and blossoms on a tree outside on a spring morning and you go from there—show him pictures of birds, or go to an aviary—that's following the child's lead." Well, to a degree. It's wonderful to satisfy a child's natural curiosity about, say, a bird. But it's important to recognize that sometimes the child just wants mom or dad to share his delight, not convert it into a learning project.

You Can Manage It All!

Why do parents feel a powerful impulse to manage so many aspects of their children's lives? Because they're good at it and because they're trained to do it.

You know those braking tests they do on automobiles? The car is going at a high rate of speed and the driver hits the brakes hard. How long does it take for the car to stop? Three feet? Five feet? There should be such a test available for new mothers. Most new moms, after all, have worked before the birth of their child. Even if they've taken some time off, they've been moving in high gear preparing for their baby. They've been decorating and shopping for onesies and interviewing pediatricians. Or, if they haven't taken time off, they've been negotiating contracts and handling staff and completing projects. Suddenly—ka-boom!—they hit the brakes. One minute they're racing at full speed and the next they're staring vacantly into space with a diaper on their shoulder. How long does it take a new mom to come to a full stop? Three days? Ten weeks? Eighteen years?

It's extremely difficult to recalibrate a lifetime of hard-won skills. It's a perplexing challenge to go from an occupation that requires, as most do, initiative, organization, and, above all, control, to an occupation that requires vast patience, empathy, and, ultimately, the relinquishment of control. Some parents never manage to make the switch. Many mothers and fathers, particularly those who continue to work, find it impossible to relax into parenting. They've learned to respect effort, hard work, success. Their buzzword is "professionalism." They have no intention, for instance, of being the old-fashioned kind of mom who shops for curtains and has the ladies over for bridge. They've gone from being a doctor or a lawyer or a sales assistant to being a MOTHER.

They can't allow themselves to be reactive; they must always be proactive. These parents take on child-rearing full bore. They research hospitals and pediatricians feverishly. They're evaluating nursery schools while they nurse. They have their deposit down on the Mommy and Me class. And as their children get older, there's far more to do, to organize. The burden is tremendous, and they feel they can't miss a step. They bring all their job skills and training—decisiveness, ability to prioritize, focus on the bottom line—to their child-rearing. They are very good at their work and they want to be very good at parenting.

I was speaking with a woman the other day when she mentioned that she was feeling totally dismayed about her parenting abilities. It seems that the sign-up date for peewee hockey had passed, and she hadn't gotten her son on the list. Now she was in a pickle: She could either try and pull some strings to get him included on the roster, or shrug her shoulders and maybe try next year. Her son didn't really seem to care—he was, after all, only seven—but she knew that it would be difficult for him to join the team a year late: The other kids would have better skills, and he would feel behind and maybe decide he didn't want to play. In that case, she would feel, it would be all her fault.

Did she know that this angst expended on mini-hockey was a little excessive? Of course she did. But, as she said, "Sometimes it feels like everyone else has a blueprint for what to do, and if you're not totally on your toes, really focused on what's around the corner, your kids will lose out."

I'm not at all unsympathetic to this impulse. All of us grew up in "consumer nation." We're used to "navigating." We're used to researching everything from the best lipstick to the best microwave. We're used to negotiating with the airlines to get a better seat. We've spent lots of time figuring out the best bank accounts and the best car deals. How could we possibly turn into "mom cows," to quote a friend, the minute we give birth? And besides, what's so wrong with wanting everything to be so right for your child?

Of course, the extreme examples of managerial moms are far more disturbing than wondering about your son's slot on pee-wee hockey. As Marlyn McGrath Lewis, director of admissions at Harvard, expressed it to *Talk* magazine, referring to the mothers of applicants, "I call it the Ralph Lauren phenomenon. It's 'I want it because I can check it off. I've bought the best clothes, the best mattress, and so I have the illusion that I can control all my other choices.'" She recognizes that these demanding moms are "accustomed to being in charge," but she points to the downside of this intensive parenting: The children are never allowed to find their own way. Lewis, who has been in her job for thirteen years, describes thus a recent crop of applicants: "Half of these kids came out of a petri dish." A headmaster at a Connecticut day school, lamenting the managerial mom type with too much time on her hands, says, "The phrase around here is 'Please let them get a job!'"

Not all managerial moms are completely over the top, of course. Most of us struggle with relatively benign questions concerning how much involvement in our children's lives is appropriate and how much is necessary. It's almost impossible not to grapple with this issue in some form. In addition to our training and our impulses, many moms who struggle with being managerial moms do so because of a very natural emotion: fear.

Consider the fact that fear is, sadly, the muted drumbeat of our times. Whether we're worrying specifically about our children or about more global issues, we are often grappling with some measure of fear.

Remember *The Worst-Case Scenario Survival Handbook*? Its astonishing success is due at least in part to its simple assurance that any situation, no matter how bizarre, unlikely, or terrifying, can be handled by taking simple steps. Shark attack? Remain calm. Hit the shark in the area of its gills or eyes where it is most sensitive to pain. Be certain to make quick, sharp, repeated jabs in these areas. Need to escape from a bear? Stay still and quiet and do not climb a tree. If it attacks, strike back, going for its eyes or snout. If we know what to do, we don't need to be fearful. If the worst happens, we'll just take certain steps and everything will be all right. Parents yearn for a "worst-case scenario" guide to parenthood. Though we know that most of us will reach the end of our parenting journey with some measure of success—our children will be happy, mature adults—we still face considerable anxiety on our fearful journey. If we could only learn how to handle every emergency, every child-rearing disaster, we'd feel in control. Learning what to do gives us the illusion of control. Action comforts us. If we know what we're supposed to do in a given situation, whether it be a bear attack or a dreadful result on a standardized test, it's not so frightening.

One of the dilemmas of parenthood, particularly when compared to many parents' recent experience in the workplace, is that there is no measure of your success. You won't really know how things turn out until it's over. This unknowing makes us feel uncomfortable, out of control. It's consoling to believe that if we take certain steps, everything will be OK. If we get our children into the right schools, make sure they excel in the right sports, help them know the right people, maybe they'll be fine. Certainly it *feels* better than doing less.

Making choices also helps us feel in control. And goodness knows, we have millions of choices to make today. Perhaps you remember how in the movie *You've Got Mail,* Tom Hanks e-mails Meg Ryan with his theory of choice in the modern world. He claims that people like buying coffee at Starbucks because, even if you can't make any real choices in your life (Get engaged? Change jobs? Start a family?), you can march up to the counter with confidence and demand a half-caff grande triple-shot nonfat latte, and feel like you're making a real choice. At last, you're able to decide! Of course, it's the *illusion* of choice. You're choosing between pink and pale salmon. But it's empowering to feel like you're the kind of person who has to have it "just so." If you can choose among a dozen beer brands, fifty kinds of olive oil, and a hundred wines, you must be in control.

One subject also relating to control that contemporary parents are obsessed with is safety. It's a primary concern. We assume that the world is a dangerous place. We are determined to keep our children out of danger. And danger is everywhere. We worry about pesticides on food, whether our cars have air bags on the sides, kitty poop in the sandbox at the playgound, and, of course, stranger danger. All of these are real concerns. But a parent's eager and anxious decision to eliminate every possible threat from a child's life is unrealistic. As David Brooks, author of *Bobos in Paradise,* points out in a recent article in *The Atlantic,* we can soon anticipate the institution of a new legal specialty: playdate law. As negotiations on what will be permitted at a playdate take on the complexity of a legal arbitration, parents struggle to assert their total ban on white sugar, while relaxing their stand on educational videos. As Brooks outlines it, ". . . the most heated talks usually revolve around safety issues. Will the nanny or parent transporting the children be using a cell phone while driving? Have all the child-safety seats recently been checked by a certified safety-seat professional? Are electrical outlets in the home protected by childproof covers? Do the oven controls have kid guards? Is there a foam bumper pad around the stone fireplace (such as the kind available through the Right Start catalogue)? What about the toilet—has it been lid-locked so that children don't accidentally fall in and drown? And the yard—has it been aerated to make the ground softer in case of falls?"

We don't want to leave anything to chance, certainly not the health or safety of our children. I am certainly not a libertarian when it comes to children and safety. After all, I work with children every day who are in the hospital because of accidents. I know, on the one hand, what it is for a parent to realize that they could have prevented an injury to their child. On the other hand, when a parent's anxiety about danger in the world translates into a controlling impulse that permeates too many aspects of the child's life, the child suffers.

I also believe that as parents we are desperately eager to do the little things: make them wear helmets, insist on air bags, work with the PTA to get the doors to the elementary school locked. It's important to do these things. However, sometimes our focus on the small things distracts us from larger issues that can have just as much, if not more, impact on our children's well-being. Divorce, for example, and exposure to violent television and movies both can be extremely difficult for children to handle even if they are less visible in their effects than a physical injury. And sometimes it's extremely hard to do the big things. As Daniel Akst pointed out in a thoughtful editorial in *The Wall Street Journal* entitled "The Parent Trap: Over-worrying Small Risks, Ignoring Big Ones," parents focus on the manageable things because they find the larger and really more important issues difficult to address. As he states, the media have exaggerated the dangers to our children (for example, the 2000 death rate statistics from accidents among children ages one to four fell an impressive 68 percent). We have fewer children, so we worry about each one more. An increase in single parenting has driven up the worry rate. But finally, as Akst says, ". . . I think the most important reason parents obsess over insignificant risks is that the significant ones are so much harder to address. It's easier to keep your child indoors than to stay married to his father, for instance, even though divorce is associated with such woes as poverty, delinquency, and impaired school performance."

So we begin parenting with a powerful impulse, generated by life experience and the fear of the unknown, to manage our children right from the beginning. Our every fear and inclination is catered to by a "parenting" industry that stands ready to make us ever more anxious, and therefore willing to spend, spend, spend to facilitate our children's success and happiness. There is an endless array of devices and services that purport to give us even more control. The implication is, as is always the case with consumerism, if we can, we should. We should buy or at least consider buying the nanny cam, the super-safe crib bumpers, the Good Housekeeping–approved outdoor play set with foam safety matting. As a result, this "industry" that caters to parents encourages two phenomena that seem to grow more pronounced with each passing year: "technotatchment" and "outsourcing parenting."

"TECHNOTACHMENT"

It begins with the nursery monitor. You're just home from the hospital. You feel bushwhacked. But you have a healthy baby and a loving husband so, except for the disorientation and fatigue, things are fine. You gently settle the baby in the bassinet and join your husband in the living room for a glass of wine— your first in ten months. Just as you put your feet on the coffee table you freeze. The nursery monitor alerts you that your baby is "snuffling." What an odd sound! Is she OK? You rush in to check. The baby is fine, of course, but you're just a tad more anxious. You'll have to make a note and ask the pediatrician about those noises. You rejoin your husband, but your ear is cocked to the plastic box. And so it begins. The nursery monitor makes us feel a bit more in control. It can be very handy when we have to be two floors away from the baby, or when the baby is sick. But, like so many technological devices, we grow dependent on it and use it all the time, even when we're in the next room and could easily hear a noise that required our attention. The result is that little snuffles and burps that years ago would have never been noticed are now the focus of attention.

Devices like nursery monitors give us the *illusion* of control. They create opportunities to intervene. They create "technotachment"—the illusion of attachment. We're not, in fact, *there* but we're on the alert to be there at a moment's notice. We *feel* like we're in control, and we feel like we should be.

Technotachment reaches its apogee when our children are older and begin to use beepers and cell phones. Suddenly, with the aid of a cell phone, a child can be in constant contact with a parent. Parents are delighted. They feel they are in touch, in control. Teens (and even children) with cell phones can be given permission to do things that we might not otherwise allow. They can go to a questionable club, stay out a bit too late, take a train alone. We are reassured because we can always reach them, and they can always reach us. It gives us a false sense of security and sometimes encourages us to put our children in situations that they perhaps shouldn't be in. It also sometimes frees us from having to set limits, pick them up, drive them somewhere ourselves, or simply find something else to occupy them. It assuages our guilt for not being with them enough. It offers them the olive branch of our trust, our love and concern. Of course it is a good thing to be able to have your child reach you by cell phone in an emergency, or facilitate soccer pickup by calling from the field. The problem comes in when we override our better judgment on restrictions and safety because we believe that a cell phone allows us more control than we in fact have.

While technotachment encourages broader freedom for children, it also fosters dependency. Many parents love the access they can have via a cell phone because they're simply not around their children very much, and it allows them a connection they wouldn't otherwise have. But this technotachment kind of connection can quickly become an unhealthy dependence as children and teens are denied opportunities to solve problems independently. A baby who is picked up the second a sound is transmitted via the baby monitor might have trouble learning to put himself to sleep. A child who is able to reach mom any time, anywhere, is likely to do so. A patient recently told me of a situation at a girls' private school that exemplifies this. A tenth-grade teacher reprimanded a child in the classroom for misbehavior. Within five minutes, two other students were excused to go to the restroom, where they both phoned their parents to report the teacher's reprimand and to complain about her. Five minutes later, the headmaster received a call from one of the parents demanding an explanation.

Without cell phones, the girls could have discussed the situation at lunch. They could have had an open debate. Perhaps they would have decided that their classmate deserved the reprimand. Perhaps they would have decided to go directly to the teacher to discuss it. Perhaps they would have discovered that the reprimanded child didn't really feel at all bothered by the situation. In any case, the hotheaded reactions of a fifteen-year-old would have been mitigated, and the teens would have learned something on their own.

Another teenage patient told of phoning her mother from a friend's house because they had had an argument, and she wanted her mother's advice on how to handle the situation. The mother felt flattered to be included in her child's life and was eager to give advice. This is a common pattern. It seems to have reached epidemic proportions in early college years. I've heard of countless instances of freshmen in college who are in constant contact with their parents, looking for help in dealing with issues ranging from roommate problems to study over-loads. Years ago, a college freshman would rarely consult with parents on these subjects and would simply cope on his own.

Technotachment also fosters the illusion of control by allowing parents to be as invasive as they like. *The Wall Street Journal* told the story of a fifteen-year-old girl who, upon exiting a Gap where she'd purchased a $149.99 black leather jacket, heard her cell phone ring. It was her mother, questioning her daughter's purchase. Despite the fact that her mother was over a hundred miles away in her office, she is attached to her daughter via PacketCard Inc., which e-mails mom instantly with details on how much her daughter spends, where she spends it, and what she spends on. As her mom said "You can't hide from me." While the PacketCard may alert parents to a purchase, it subverts the more helpful give and take that encourages young people to learn about money and appropriate spending habits. A teenager might find it more beneficial, if certainly more annoying, to have to discuss in advance what she'd like to buy and how much it might cost. While the device saves the parent the time and agony of debating the current price of t-shirts, it also eliminates a potentially valuable parent-child interchange.

"OUTSOURCING PARENTING"

As the managerial mom tries to stay abreast of all the child-rearing demands and perhaps a busy work, volunteer, and social life, she finds that while she can do the "work"-related part of it—the phone calls, the on-line research, the networking—it's very hard to do the actual hands-on parenting. She doesn't have enough time. And she doesn't feel she can really do the nitty-gritty part as well as someone else. She may not be a great cook or costume maker or party planner. She realizes that the only way to manage it all is to do what she'd do at work: out-source it. So she begins to outsource parenting, and she's encouraged at every step in this effort by the same parenting industry that's so eager to sell her devices. Now they can sell her expertise.

More and more of what our children learn they learn not from us but from paid help. From classes in table manners and etiquette to SAT tutors and specialized sports coaches, we hand over our children with the hope and belief that the professionals will do a better job than we ever could. We begin to parent by remote control, and we find that it's easier, more "professional," and probably more "effective."

The *New York Times* reported on a professional bike-riding tutor in Westchester who delights parents by taking the hassle out of teaching their kids to ride two-wheelers. His tutoring has proved so successful and popular that he has expanded his services. Now, in addition to offering private lessons to children in elementary school and tips on how to switch to mountain bikes for older children and adults [tip: get your parents to buy you one], he is now offering "playdate" bike lessons for two or three youngsters at a time. As the article pointed out, in a culture where children routinely get extra help with academic subjects, receive private coaching in sports to enhance their potential to make a team, and take private music lessons to supplement school instruction, it's not surprising that learning to ride a bike has also become something for professionals to handle. As one mom said, "Some things children learn better from professionals. Just because I can ride a bike myself, doesn't mean I can teach it."

Many parents, in their zeal to do the best for their children in a competitive world, forget that for children the valuable part of Dad teaching you to ride a bike or Mom making a birthday cake with you is *simply being with a parent.* Children, at least until they're teenagers, yearn to be with us, and they do better psychologically when they *are* with us. During World War II, when London was being bombed, many children were moved to the countryside to escape the terrors of the bombing. Follow-up studies of this perhaps extreme example found that children who had experienced the blitz with their parents were actually in better psychological shape than those who had been sent to live in a calmer environment. This was because those who re-mained in the city were with their parents. Surely our mis-guided efforts at a birthday party or a bike riding lesson couldn't be any more traumatic than the London blitz.

Related to outsourcing parenting is another area of our chil-dren's lives where we seem quite eager to cede control: their gathering of "experience" independent from their family life. We seem to believe that a cross-country car trip or vacation at the beach doesn't do for a child what a "professional" experience can do. Standing in line at one of my children's schools in September, I struck up a conversation with a twelve-year-old whom I knew casually. Asking about her summer, I learned that she had gone to Japan to study art for a month and also to a "leadership" camp for a few weeks. These had been fantastic "experiences" in her view, even though when it came to the de-tails of how she had spent her time in these travels, it didn't sound like all that much fun. She had hated having to soak in a large tub in Japan after showering, and had been quite home-sick on both the Japan trip and the camping trip.

The kind of travel that can be exciting and delightful for children (and even teenagers) when experienced with their own family can be unnerving and even frightening when alone.

It's curious how we have become so accustomed to dismissing the downsides of these kinds of "experiences" our children endure. Our own normal worry about, for example, a young child taking a plane flight without her parents is tamped down in favor of the supposed benefit of the trip to the child. Children have been flying alone for decades, and airlines have done their best to accommodate young solos. Nonetheless, stories of girls getting their first period on board, and school-age children wetting their pants or burning their tongues on hot meals are routine. By the time the child gets home, the mishap is often forgotten, and the homesickness, which has become transformed into a "growth experience," is ancient history. The airlines are now beginning to refuse to take solo minors; they know some things that parents don't.

What's wrong with technotachment and outsourcing parenting? We lose out on a joyful and meaningful connection with our children. We miss opportunities to share with them experiences that are important to us. But most significant and most damaging to our children, we miss the point. By focusing on the goal, the end result, we ignore the most important part of parenting: the process.

We also increase our own sense of ultimate and potentially devastating responsibility for the outcome. After all, once you define a goal in parenting, you can't help but analyze the results. Thus the inevitable "uh-oh" moments when we feel that we've really messed up terribly and irrevocably in some area of child-rearing. We've all been there: Suddenly you realize that you should have insisted that little Cara continue with soccer, because now she's been ostracized from her formerly tight group of friends who are all having sleepovers after games. You should have signed Sam up for piano lessons because the best teacher in town now has no openings. Many mothers live with a constant vague sense of anxiety—the "cloud of could"—that they are not "keeping up" in some way that will matter greatly to their children in the future.

We all have a tremendous impulse to blame ourselves when something goes wrong for our children. The force of this guilt and blame has been magnified today as we assume more and more responsibility for our children's various sports, social activities, tutors, and enrichment lessons. And of course it's not just that we assume the complex calculus of scheduling all these activities; we also assume, to some degree, responsibility for their outcome. Every class, sport, or birthday party becomes a small neutron bomb of potential failure.

When we put all this energy, time, and yes, money into our children's day-to-day lives, we expect what anyone working with a business model expects: We want a return on investment. We want results. If we've struggled to get our son a spot on the peewee hockey team; we've invested so much in the equipment that we're embarrassed to even tell our own parents what it's costing; and we've devoted weekend after weekend to games and practices, we want to see him out there playing and playing well. We didn't do all this to watch him warm the bench.

"I hear families use the word *packaging,*" says the mother of a high school senior at one of the city's most competitive girls' schools. Commenting in a recent article in *New York* magazine, she's referring to the college application process and the use of private counselors who work to get students admitted to the colleges of their choice. " 'We're packaging our daughter.' The hair stands up on the back of your neck. They made an investment, and they want a return." In the same article, John Katzman, head of *Princeton Review,* observes, "You have these parents who are very business- and result-oriented. In the same way they expect someone who works for them to work all night and close the deal, they approach their kids like a subordinate whose job is to get into Harvard. At any given moment when the kid is doing something off-strategy, like dating, the parent is all over them and saying, 'What haven't you done today to get the Harvard account?' "

Children pick up on our intensity and determination to have them succeed, and when they're young they desperately want to please us. It's truly agonizing to watch small children participate in activities that they hate because they're simply too afraid to tell their parents they want to stop. Or because they have completely buried their own feelings and are plodding joylessly through yet another soccer season. One orthopedic specialist I know tells me that he frequently sees young athletes who have been injured in action on the playing field from activity that is simply too much for their young bodies. Sometimes, he says, he asks the parents to leave the room, and it's not uncommon for the child to say that he doesn't want to continue with the sport but is afraid to tell his parents. This kind of performance pressure routinely backfires in adolescence, as I'll describe in the second part of the book. But it's very clear that parental investment and the desire to see a return heightens the anxiety levels of parent and child, both of whom are trapped on the escalator marked "achievement."

The upshot of all this anxiety and guilt is that much of child-rearing becomes a tremendous, joyless burden. If only *you* can make it happen, then only *you* are responsible when it doesn't! It's no wonder that many of us have occasional dark moments of real resentment toward our children. The more we assume the burden of their success, the more we feel the pain of their failures. As one young woman reported in an article in the *New*

York Times, her rejections from Ivy League colleges were felt "as a death in the family" by her parents.

As our children are being managed and perfected with expert help, travel experiences, and classes, we become, whether we know it or not, increasingly anxious and stressed out. Even the satisfaction of producing accomplished children with impressive résumés is small reward when a tiny voice is telling us that we've sacrificed our role as teacher and protector, and we've squandered the only truly valuable thing that we have: time.

Money Equals Happiness

We want our children to be happy and, at first glance, it seems the quickest route to happiness is money.

There is nothing closer to a parent's heart than the health and happiness of their child. If you ask a pregnant mother about her child-to-be, she will usually say, "I only ask that it's healthy," and she certainly means it. If you ask the parent of an older child what they would wish for their child's future, most would claim the happiness of that child would be their biggest wish. But if you listen closely, there's less assurance in this chorus. As the years go by and "happiness" replaces "health" at the top of a parent's wish list, things become more complicated. What actually is "happy"? Where does it come from? Libraries have been filled with attempts to answer these elusive questions. There is no one answer for everyone. But it's useful to pause and think about happiness in connection with our goals for our children.

First, I think we can all assume that happiness is a worthy goal, even if we recognize that it's not something we can pursue like a great tennis serve. We recognize that we can't insure the future health of our children besides feeding them well, keeping them active, and paying scrupulous attention to their medical care. But what about their future happiness? We tend to deconstruct it into tangible pieces that we can control and work on right now. Academic success might well affect their future financial success and ultimately their happiness. That's something we can work on right now. Or so we can believe. So if happiness is a worthy goal, and even our Declaration of Independence names the pursuit of happiness as one of our human rights, then how do we get there, or more to the point, how do we get our kids there?

Too often we rely on the closest, loudest voice to define happiness. That voice is clear to a five-year-old or a ten-year-old: Happiness is what you get with money. Lots and lots of money. Anyone can see that. If you have a lot of money, you have a lot of toys and candy and a big TV and you go on trips to Disney World and you can buy all the clothes you want and have a computer in your room and never have to share. I recently saw a board game called "Who's the Richest?" The package was marked "not suitable for children under thirty-six months due to small parts." Perhaps they're working on the version for infants.

As children grow older, the pressure becomes even more insistent. Eventually, around the fifth grade, or even earlier in some environments, children begin to compare themselves to their peers. They begin to appreciate material differences and learn about brand names. "Max has a pool table and a Jacuzzi.

We just have a pool." "Jessica has a Range Rover but we only have a Land Rover." "Josh took a private jet to Jackson Hole to ski. Max drove to ski in Vermont." They begin to appreciate that Judy's family vacation was at that fancy resort with a giant water slide, and Jack spent the holiday at home in his backyard.

As children continue to grow, their pressure for more and more becomes ever more difficult for a parent to shrug off. Now it's radiating out from the community, and it's dragging us into the fray. While the fourth-grader with the best backpack is pretty far below the parental radar screen, the fifth-grader with the best and most lavish birthday party is harder to ignore. I know a fourth-grader who attended a birthday party held at a mall. Each child was given fifty dollars and the activity was to shop for yourself. Who needs pin the tail on the donkey? Or perhaps they've heard about the FAO Schwarz "Ultimate Sleepover Adventure," which, for seventeen thousand dollars, offers an in-store slumber party for fifteen friends, and includes a backpack filled with goodies, a midnight treasure hunt, a DVD movie, and a one-hundred-dollar store gift certificate. Now our children may find their social lives affected by our responses to these pressures for more, bigger, and better. One parent I know was shocked to realize her sixth-grader didn't want to invite a friend to a sleepover because the child felt that their home wasn't up to snuff.

All of our children today have been exposed to the most competitive and intense levels of acquisition seen in generations. Most are keenly aware of designer labels, second and third homes, and car prices, even if their parents have no interest in these things. If they watch television, they see shows in which fine distinctions between monetary values are the context for jokes, conversations, and even plot devices. If they don't know the difference between Mudd, Guess?, Calvin Klein, and Big Star jeans, they will soon learn.

A fifteen-year-old was brought in to see me by her mother, who was concerned about a change in her daughter's eating habits. Upon meeting the teen, who looked attractive and healthy, I learned that she had gained ten pounds since the beginning of school. This weight enraged her mother, who said, "I spent thousands on her school wardrobe, and I am not buying her another t-shirt until she drops those pounds." This was a troubling reaction because her daughter wasn't yet fully developed and could anticipate gaining a few more pounds before her growth chart leveled off. The daughter, for her part, was less concerned about the weight gain, but had inherited her mother's keen sense of consumerism. She clarified the distinction between DKNY and Donna Karan, confiding her favorite was the latter, as DKNY was "second-best."

One recent *New York Times* article quotes an eighteen-year-old Long Island high school senior as she ticks off her recent shopping acquisitions: "I own a Prada messenger bag. I have two Kate Spades, a Gucci belt, and a Prada belt, and several pairs of Sisley jeans. I have a lot of Clinique makeup, Bobbi Brown eyeliner, MAC lip gloss, and Angel perfume—that's by Thierry Mugler." These items were bought with last summer's lifeguard salary; they were not the indulgences of affluent parents or relatives.

Certainly the quotation above confirms a comment made by Susan Faludi in a recent *Newsweek* editorial about the commercialization of feminism: "In a consumer culture, economic independence became 'getting ahead,' human potential became 'having it all,' and choice became the right to choose liposuction."

———

This constant pressure from our children can make even the most confirmed aesthete rethink her priorities or at least grudgingly, distractedly accept the idea that, yes, the more money the better. After all, for many parents, it's been years since they expected to find perfect happiness in their job, or their community, or even their mate. Their child is the closest they've come to unalloyed delight, so if money and more and more "things" make this source of such pleasure—the beloved child—so happy, perhaps attention must be paid.

Even noncompetitive, nonmaterialistic parents get drawn into the fray. They often come to see a child's interest in material things as an access route to winning the child's favor. We may not have time for our kids, but we do have money, and it relieves the guilt we feel about not being around because of divorce or work.

Certainly the general cultural shift has taken us from the altruistic "ask not what your country can do for you . . ." sixties to the "he whose children has the most toys wins" new century.

It's not news to any parent that competitive consumption reigns supreme in most of our cities and suburbs. Despite the fact that the average family size is decreasing, the average house built today is nearly twice as big as those built in the fifties. And they're crammed full with stuff and wired for DSL and surround sound. We feel pressure to own DVDs, Palm Pilots, VCRs, laptops, MiniDisc players, mountains of sports equipment, and the biggest gas-guzzling SUV that will fit in the garage (to tote as much of this stuff as possible on ski trips, weekend getaways, shopping trips to buy yet more stuff). It's interesting to note that although "developing a philosophy of life" was a top goal for most Americans in the sixties, by the late seventies that goal had changed to "attaining financial success." In the American Council on Education's annual survey of over two hundred thousand entering college students, the proportion agreeing that an important reason for their going to college was "to make more money" rose from one in two in 1971 to nearly three in four by 1990. The number who considered it very important or essential that they become "very well off financially," rose from 39 percent in 1970 to 74 percent in 1990.

We boomer parents in particular grew up believing that a philosophy of life was crucial and still give that notion lip service. Many of us, however, send complicated mixed messages to our kids, who are well aware that our drive to insure their ability to achieve professional success competes with our hope that they find lasting love and fulfillment in their work, or make a meaningful contribution to society.

Not only our children pressure us to accept money as our true master. Our culture, which increasingly is becoming the global culture, tells us at every turn that money will make us happy. Pause for a moment to reflect that the job of advertising is to make us *unhappy*—unhappy with our décor, our car, our bodies, our toothpaste, our brand of coffee. Everywhere we look, something is telling us that if we spend more money our lives could be better, more fun, more fulfilling. The choices are unlimited; the pressure is on!

And we're trying to keep up, but for many of us it's not working. In a 1995 Merck Family Fund poll, more than a quarter of those in households with incomes of more than one hundred thousand dollars a year said that they couldn't afford to buy what they really needed. That's right, not the extras but what they really *needed*. This is sadly contrary to what so many

Americans believe: that economic hardship isn't about race or class; it's about character. Presumably, if you read the right self-help books, put your furniture in the right corner of the room, heed the exortions of the of the latest CNN money guru, adopt the right twelve-step program, and demonstrate a little determination—badda-badda-bing—you're rich!

It is extremely difficult to drown out the sound and the effect of money on children without conscious effort on the part of a parent.

It's easy to see how we, as parents, as workers, as consumers, become fatally infected with money lust. And if we do believe that money is the route to happiness, then it's important to push our children toward the path that will yield the greatest riches. Many of us believe, if only reflexively, that the most direct path to the pot of gold includes four years in an Ivy League college as a crucial pit stop. So in order to get on the right track, we have to start with the right nursery school, which will perhaps mean that we better invest in those Mozart tapes once the first sonogram comes back. We assume that an ivy-covered diploma will guarantee our child a privileged, wealthy life. But to sidestep the route to wealth, for the moment, let's just take a look at what we know about what really does make people happy.

To jump to the heart of the matter: Does money make people happy? The simple answer is no. No research has shown that lots of money is a significant contributor to happiness. Of course, *some* money is critical to happiness. What does this mean? It means that once we have our basic needs met, that is, food, housing, physical comfort, and human connections, we have all we need to be happy. Poverty is not romantic and does not contribute in any way to general happiness. In fact, poverty is time and again one of the greatest risk factors for disability and disease. So for starving people living in desperate conditions, money can buy nutrition and health—and certainly that is a step toward happiness.

As University of Illinois psychologist Ed Diener, who has studied the effect of wealth on happiness, explains it, at the bottom of the scale—say in countries where people make less than ten thousand dollars a year—basic improvements like education, nutrition, healthcare, and human rights make a big difference in people's overall happiness. But once a nation is developed, its people's reported happiness stays remarkably constant. The bottom line is, as David G. Myers states it in his exhaustively researched *The Pursuit of Happiness,* once beyond poverty, further economic growth does not appreciably improve human morale. It simply does not follow that lots of money brings even greater happiness.

Indeed, in my work, I find that lots of money—too much money—is also a risk factor for disability and disease of a psychological nature. The film *Traffic* brilliantly portrays how children of preoccupied, wealthy parents are at risk for parental neglect and have the cash on hand (and the access to cars) to do serious damage with drugs and alcohol. Erika Christensen plays the daughter of a complacent Ohio judge portrayed by Michael Douglas. As Douglas prepares to take over as the nation's new "drug czar," his pampered, high-achieving daughter, unbeknownst to him, is inhaling crack at preppie parties in their wealthy suburb.

I once had as a patient a fifteen-year-old boy whose parents were divorced. The mother, a highly placed executive, was transferred to Paris. The boy was sent to live with his father so that he wouldn't have to change schools. But the father's work demanded a great deal of travel to Asia. The boy was left for prolonged periods with a Guatemalan housekeeper. He was brought to my office when he was seriously involved in smoking dope, including crack, stealing, and spending increasing amounts of time clubbing.

Are mothers happier than they were ten or fifteen years ago? According to a study, "Women's Voices 2000," conducted by the Center for Policy Alternatives, they are not. As Linda Tarr-Whelan, president of the CPA, said, "In 1992 the economy was rotten, but women were optimistic." After nearly a decade of an improving economy and higher standards of living all around, women, when asked about their current state of mind, responded with words like "angry," "awful," "sick," and "fed up." As the survey summed it up: "Women are asking, 'Is this as good as it gets?' "

It seems that one of the major flaws in seeking wealth as a source of happiness is that we are, if nothing else, adaptable. In this context, adaptability is a drag: We adjust quickly to each new level of wealth we achieve and the pleasure it brings can soon evaporate. I refer to this as the purse theory—things expand to fill up whatever volume is available. If you buy a handbag half the size of Texas, you can bet that in about three days it will be chock-full of stuff.

It's thrilling to get a big raise or bonus. But human nature is such that we soon spend it or adjust to it by buying steak instead of chicken or ground round, Prada instead of Polo or Price Club, or maybe by just saving it. In any event, we're soon thinking there must be something more, maybe something better. Certainly that's the operative impulse in the mind of the five-year-old who is becoming bored with her tenth Barbie before she's even lost the little shoes.

Most readers of this book have enough to be fed and warm.

For us, the critical question is: How much more than enough is enough? Or, will a Mercedes make us, and our children, happier than a Honda? Should we wish them riches? Should we do everything in our power to make their lives cushy and to guide them toward the greatest possible material gain? Well, as Seneca, Rome's leading intellectual figure, observed nearly two thousand years ago

> "Our forefathers . . . lived every jot as well as we, when they provided and dressed their own meat with their own hands, lodged upon the ground and were not as yet come to the vanity of gold and gems . . . which may serve to show us, that it is the mind, and not the sum, that makes any person rich . . . No one can be poor that has enough, nor rich, that covets more than he has."

There are countless versions of this sentiment. Some, like Seneca's, are based on philosophy; others, like this condensed version from the Hebrew text "Ethics of Our Fathers," are based on religious tradition: "Who is a rich man? He who is happy with his lot."

Reading these sensible words of Seneca's or from Judaism won't change us: Most of us still want as much as we can get. (Our view is less Seneca and more Ben Affleck's character in the film *Boiler Room:* "Anybody who tells you money is the root of all evil never had any.") But it may be worthwhile as parents to recognize that what will make our children happy probably is *not* money, and probably is, to some degree, under our control. Because what we know about happiness is that it is, largely, in your head. Most of us recognize this when we've had a "near-miss" experience that temporarily realigns our blurred vision. We narrowly escape a plane or car crash, a loved one is tentatively diagnosed with a critical illness that is then reversed, our biopsy comes back clear. During those minutes, hours, days of uncertainty, we reassess our life. What is insignificant falls away; what's left is the core, the key to our happiness. But even those who do not get away unscathed benefit from the experience. Here are two telling examples:

- A study of Michigan car accident victims found that three weeks after they suffered a paralyzing spinal cord injury happiness was again their prevailing emotion.

- In their interviews with dozens of breast cancer patients, UCLA health psychologists Shelley Taylor and Rebecca Collins discovered that many claimed to have benefited from their experience.

Of course, this is not to suggest that tragedy breeds happiness or contentment. But it does tell us that there is something in the human spirit that seeks happiness *regardless* of tangible factors, be they wealth, appearances, or even physical ease. And that being able to keep our lives in perspective is a critical piece of the happiness puzzle.

If we want our children to be happy, we can help them achieve that goal right now. Countless books and research studies have been devoted to the exploration of what, in fact, makes people happy. Most of the sources of genuine happiness must be understood in relation to concepts such as character, virtue, community, and service. In general, most theorists agree with the following traits of happy people:

- They like themselves.

- They feel in control of most aspects of their lives.

- They have hope even when they don't feel in control.

- They are outgoing.

If we try to help our children develop these traits, we'll have a much greater effect on their achievement of happiness than if our focus is solely on guiding our children toward economic success.

Media Life Equals Real Life

The models we look to for inspiration on how to lead our daily lives have changed. Forget the lady down the street and Aunt Jane in Pennsylvania: If all those people on TV and in the magazines can have such impressive, accomplished, high-octane families, why can't we?

Once upon a time, in the beginning and middle of the last century, people looked to their neighbors and friends, teachers and clergy, literature and history for illustrations of how to live. There were commonly accepted tenets of family life and, though they changed through the years, the basic ideals of behavior were unquestioned and could be observed across the block and across town. You should be honest, kind, compassionate, prompt, brave, and so on. People functioned in a community of others who provided a touchstone for behavior. You bumped into people at the post office, at weddings, at town meetings. You gossiped about the girl who disappeared for nine months and came home chastened, the mother who was extraordinarily lax about housekeeping, and the father who could be found in the tavern most weekends. If you leafed through a pile of *Saturday Evening Post*s from the fifties, you'd be amazed at what a provincial world that magazine portrays. With stories about the local 4-H club winner in Illinois and the veteran who was chosen Teacher of the Year in Iowa, the articles seem like distant echoes of a storybook culture.

Television changed all that. Television changed everything. Television has been the prime mover in creating a cult of celebrity and transforming the way we see our lives. The single biggest effect of life with TV is that people no longer judge themselves against the people across the street, but against the celebrity on the coffee table. Indeed, some people feel they have a closer relationship with TV personalities than with members of their own, perhaps distant, families, and certainly a closer relationship than the one they have with their neighbors, some of whom they rarely if ever see.

The phenomenon of "real life on TV" has further blurred the line between real life and media life. We all know Oprah, Rosie, Katie, and those gals on *The View*. We think of them as friends and admire them with good reason: Oprah's booklist has gotten many people reading and joining a dialogue about important issues, and Rosie's natural appearance and lack of pretension are a wake-up call to over-processed celebrities. The *Today* show on NBC has found that individual anchors can inspire such loyalty to the show that they keep the ratings high year after year. It's not necessarily the show's content; it's the personalities of the hosts that make us want to invite them into our homes daily, observe their hairstyle changes, and keenly note any glimmerings we can get of their personal lives. There's a warm pseudorelationship that exists between the viewer and the "personalities," and it makes the conversation, the advice, and the encouragement seem far more real, emphatic, and useful than the advice we receive from actual friends. Oprah has benefited from this relationship like no one else. Her magazine and her show have made her into a kind of pop cultural evangelist, encouraging women to be their best selves in a way ("You go, girl!") that their mothers and friends used to. Rosie O'Donnell challenges some shallow aspects of this pseudorelationship, as she's noted in various interviews connected with the release of her magazine. She finds it disconcerting when people in the supermarket are disappointed that she's not always smiling. As she says, the expression she wears on her show is her "game face." But her audience seems to feel betrayed when she insists that the person she is on the show is not the real Rosie. The viewers insist that it is.

Of course, the truth is we don't really—nor should we—know how Katie Couric feels about losing her husband to colon cancer, though we imagine we do. And we don't know what her relationship with her children is like. We're not reminded that beautiful, laughing Julia Roberts is appearing on a talk show not because she likes us and wants to share with us but because she is starring in a recently released movie and wants us to come and see it and keep her film fees in the stratosphere. And that the editor from a parenting magazine is there not because she really found the very best way to get your child to sleep through the night but because the producers know that this is a persistent problem for parents, and if you believe she has the solution, you'll buy her magazine.

What we do know, or what we come to appreciate over endless hours of television watching, is that the people we see on TV live lives that seem better, glossier, and smoother than ours.

They have time to exercise in the morning with a trainer. They never mention cleaning their bathrooms. They have super relationships with their spouses and children. Why can't our husbands be a bit more like Mel Gibson, who juggles millions of dollars, glamorous roles, international travel, and cheerful hands-on baby care? And what about Susan Sarandon: fulfilling career, political causes, lots of money, happy family, no wrinkles, doting partner? Isn't that what our middle age ought to look like?

Of course all we really get from TV is what TV wants us to have. Certainly the sitcom and TV-movie world that can be so absorbing and relaxing is far from real. The people are beautiful. Their kitchens are sparkling. The weather is perfect except when it's awful. Certainly the high quality of New York apartments inhabited by marginally employed characters like Kramer and Jerry Seinfeld in *Seinfeld* hint that their world is not our world. But we don't feel much impulse to check behind the curtain; it's too much fun to just watch. We accept that the Odd Couple, Oscar and Felix, lived together year after year without arousing suspicions and that "Friends" don't really have to work, at least not very hard.

In fact, American culture changes, or tries to change, to match the world on TV. The shows that are "cutting edge" in their time—from *All in the Family* to *The Sopranos*—introduce social issues such as homosexuality, abortion, cancer, etc., to a public that perhaps has not been quite ready to explore them. But Archie Bunker's and Tony Soprano's reactions to these issues give us clues on how we too can and should react. Murphy Brown, the single, pregnant, recovering-alcoholic news anchor, gave us a new slant on deviance. Perhaps if the woman down the block were in similar straits, we'd have a more conservative reaction to the situation, but when it's framed by Candice Bergen's appealing personal strength, suddenly single motherhood seems like an admirable role. (Indeed, when Murphy Brown rebuffed then Vice President Dan Quayle on the show after he had publicly rebuked the character, she drew 44 million viewers, a larger audience than watched the Republican convention—that boring, droning, real-life piece of anti-entertainment—one month earlier.)

This isn't all bad. Television opens topics for discussion that might forever remain closed in some households and serves as a useful educational tool. But it can't be denied that it plays a powerful role in how we view ourselves. And its heroes and their behavior, from Madonna's sexually explicit videos to Michael Jackson's androgynous sexuality to Tony Soprano's casual relation with the law, affect the way we see cultural mores and the way we embrace or reject social standards. Television moves us along much faster than the collective opinion of the neighborhood would.

If we've abandoned the neighborhood in our search for heroes and models, if the fireman and the college professor and the successful local businesswoman won't do, we still can't help but sense that there's quite a gap between the way we live and the way celebrities supposedly live. It's a challenge to measure up to the people we see on the small screen. Maybe our daughter doesn't look up to us the way Kate Hudson does to Goldie Hawn. Maybe our pregnancy wasn't the dream trip that Cindy Crawford's was.

But it's a little late for us anyway. We're willing to acknowledge that it may be unrealistic to think that we could achieve the looks and seemingly full lives of celebrities, but perhaps our kids can do better . . . At least that's the message that creeps in like smoke under the doorjamb. There are lots of role models. Tara Lipinski became a U.S. Olympic skating champion just two weeks after her twelfth birthday and soon had the *New York Times, Sports Illustrated,* and *Dateline,* among others, knocking at her door. At age thirteen, she already had an agent to handle her endorsements and appearances. We all see and read about the children who are Olympic hopefuls, successful child actors, and musical prodigies and still somehow manage to get excellent grades and volunteer at the local soup kitchen. The morning shows are filled with youngsters who are astonishingly accomplished in some fashion while still seeming to retain the humility and appeal of a young Gregory Peck or Ingrid Bergman. My son's laid-back summer camp sends a newsletter in advance of the season to introduce new campers. This year for the first time, the new campers are described in Dewar's Profile terms: "Megan Jones from New Canaan loves horseback riding, has a brown belt in karate, plays the violin and flute, and is looking forward to learning to water ski." Megan is a sweet and friendly girl, and to a person who knows the real child, reading this description of her makes her in some way unreal, a list of stats more appropriate to a competition than an introduction.

To some degree, as we become swamped with these images—images of children who are preternaturally accomplished and poised—we gradually lose the realistic appreciation of what childhood really is. When the boy down the road, little Tommy Jones, gets a MacArthur Grant and is all over the media, we know, because we've watched him grow up, the truth about Tommy: that he spent years as a goofball—the despair of his parents—before he straightened out and pulled himself together. Or, when someone in our town, little Mary Smith, wins acclaim as a brilliant musician, we know that she worked for years and years to achieve her position and perhaps gave up other satisfactions in the pursuit of her goal. And that there were perhaps times when she wondered if it all was worth it. We see the price of celebrity. And we see how fleeting it is when a year later we see Mary Smith working as a substitute teacher because she's between jobs. We see the beginning, middle, and end of fame and accomplishment. But when we only see one part out of context—the TV, *People* magazine part—when strangers leap out of ordinary life and onto the media pedestal, we're dazzled because it looks so easy, so perfect, so doable.

With the media world an ever-stronger influence on our lives, we feel the impulse to wonder, quite unconsciously, why our own little family isn't more, well, polished and accomplished. Sometimes we even lose the ability to see our own children in the moment as their own little selves. We can become preoccupied trying to improve them and burnish them into what we've come to assume are "better" children. In the worst instances, we sometimes begin to see our children only in terms of their accomplishments. The more skilled, lauded, and beribboned, the better. We begin to devalue what's in our own living rooms, our own lives.

It's not just the parents who sometimes unconsciously absorb television values and apply them to their own family situations. Our children are way ahead of us in their total immersion in TV and media culture. After all, we can only guess how many hours they've spent watching the box ever since the soothing words of Mr. Rogers bought us five minutes of peace years ago. The most pervasive example of the effect of TV on America's youth is their language patterns. Do you remember that there was once a time before "like" was a reflexive punctuation in every other phrase a teen utters? Before *Beverly Hills 90210* children spoke much like adults at least in terms of sentence structure and phrasing. Now, they, like, don't. Whatever. While certainly teens of the past had their own slang, the "Valley-speak" that invaded youth culture years ago and stayed is far more than a few popular phrases: It's actually a modified speech pattern. I'm not arguing the positive or negative impact of a phrase or two, but I do think the fact that contemporary speech patterns of young people have been altered is noteworthy and emblematic of the power of the media.

Children also adopt the behavior, morals, goals, and appearance of popular television stars. Many activities and obsessions that mystify parents have their roots in television. Have you noticed how teens, even sometimes middle-school students, want to hire limousines for parties and dances? How it's become routine for young girls to have their nails done professionally? And how younger and younger girls feel quite comfortable dancing like MTV video stars? A recent commercial for an odd toy—tiny shoes that you wear on your fingers and dance in, tabletop-style—features a trio of prepubescent girls who bump and grind with abandon.

The most troubling aspect of the pervasive media is the glamorization of violence and the resulting negative effect of this upon children. There is no question that violence on television, whether it's a cable movie, a kiddie cartoon, or a "real-life drama," arouses a child's identification, usually with the hero or aggressor, desensitizes a child to the accurate consequences of violence, and trivializes human suffering. Overall, media violence teaches children that aggression is an effective and acceptable means of conflict resolution. If it's a dog-eat-dog world on TV, it isn't too much of a stretch before it's the same at home.

So what's a parent to do? Turn off the TV? It's not that simple or easy. But I think it's important to at least recognize the effect that television and the media are having on our child-rearing habits and the way we look at our own children. Of course, culture is always in flux, and television will play a major role in influencing change. There's no escape from that. But we do control what goes on in our own heads, and we can work toward a more personal and individual view of our children and our families.

Certainly, in our efforts to improve our children, to bring them up to some "national above-average standard," we lose out on the satisfaction we could be taking from the process of raising our very own unique offspring. As I mentioned in regard to the previous myth of money equaling happiness, actual income doesn't much influence happiness—how satisfied we are with our income does. To some degree this holds true for our relationships with our children. The child's résumé doesn't much matter; it's how we feel about the child. If we are routinely comparing them to an ideal—a bogus, buffed, media-generated ideal—we are bound to live with nagging dissatisfaction as they fail to measure up. If we see them as OK the way they are—sometimes wonderful, sometimes way less than perfect—we can't help but be happier and better parents.

Mirror, Mirror on the Wall, You're the Greatest Mom of All!

Sometimes we identify so strongly with our children that we have trouble separating our needs from theirs. We push because their success becomes our success and it's intoxicating.

"Mirror, mirror on the wall, who's the greatest mom of all?" Just imagine Glenn Close playing the Queen in the twisted, modern version of *Snow White*, so consumed with her ability as a parent that she is oblivious to her child's real needs. She spends her days in the castle, phoning tutors and coaches, gazing in her mirror. She lives in terror of the mirror's wrong response—that one day she'll *really* see her child stumbling out of the middle-school cafeteria with a poor report card, not many friends, and not a single extra-curricular.

It's hard to separate from your child and hard for your child to separate from you. Indeed, it's the major task of parenting and of growing up. Too many parents today are seduced into identifying so strongly with their children that they behave in ways that are unhealthy and ultimately damaging to their children's ability to develop into strong, independent, and mature adults.

As a mother, you and your baby begin life together in every way. At conception, you *are* one. At birth, you are at least physically separated, but most mothers and children are never totally separated emotionally. The bond between parent and child, particularly between mother and child, is powerful in the early weeks and months of life. Few pleasures match the feeling of a newborn asleep on your chest. Many new mothers cry at their infants' first inoculations. But eventually a healthy separation begins, and the parent is able to distinguish her feelings from those of her child. You wince when your two-year-old gets a shot, but you don't lose your grip as you hold him still. You recognize that your child isn't old enough to see certain movies, so you insist she doesn't, despite her pleading. You may insist that your child write a thank-you note even though he's tired, and even though you could do it for him in a minute. You refuse to let your young teen go clubbing in the city, even when she's screaming that you're the reason she has no friends and she's never going to speak to you again.

Bruno Bettelheim describes thus this critical component of good parental decision-making: "Good-enough parents endeavor to evaluate and respond to matters both from their adult perspective and from the quite different one of the child, and to base their actions on a reasonable integration of the two, while accepting that the child, because of his immaturity, can understand matters only from his point of view."

The healthy development of an infant demands interplay between the mother and baby, and the balance of the interplay is always in flux. D. W. Winnicott, the renowned psychoanalytic theorist, made crucial contributions to our understanding of this particular area of child development. Decades ago, he observed that, "The good-enough mother . . . starts off with an almost complete adaptation to her infant's needs, and, as time proceeds, she adapts less and less completely, gradually, according to the infant's growing ability to deal with her failure . . ." In other words, the mother initially anticipates and fulfills as best she can every single one of her baby's needs. But as the infant begins to mature, the mother changes as well: Sensing her baby's growing ability to manipulate the world and also to handle frustration, she begins to demand that the child do more. "You can pick up that pacifier yourself, can't you?" "You'll have to wait one minute for that bottle while Mommy finishes this chore." "I think you're big enough to pour your own juice now, don't you?"

I have a short list of questions about milestones, which I use when I work with parents. The answers I get clue me in to this process between parent and child. They include: When did your baby first hold his/her own bottle? When did he/she get out of bed by him/herself after a full night's sleep? And not head straight to your room? When did he/she first go to the bathroom unaccompanied? When did he/she first fix his own cereal? Make his/her own grilled cheese sandwich? Wait for the bus alone? Of course, every child and parent's timetable is different, but it is useful to know when children begin to take on more independence.

"Mirroring" is the term used to describe what Winnicott observed. The parent, in this view, serves as a kind of mirror to the baby. When the infant looks in the mother's face, he is looking for a reflection of himself. The mother "mirrors" back what she sees in the baby's face, duplicating the sounds baby makes, smiling when baby smiles, sticking her tongue out as baby does the same, and so forth. Most parents instinctively engage in this dynamic mirroring from their first moments with their infant, and most parents instinctively know when the mirroring can become more demanding and complex. A mother would probably not feel inclined to play "peekaboo" with a week-old baby: An infant of this age is unable to grasp or even be interested in the concept of Mom disappearing and returning again. But when a baby is nine months old, peekaboo has become a delightful game.

The critical aspect of mirroring is picking up on when our child is ready for the next step, and when we're ready to, as Winnicott put it, "adapt less and less completely" to our child's needs. As parents, we have to be the "frontal lobes" of the operation for our children—the decision-making part. The frontal lobes of our brain help us assess and reflect on a situation, delay actions or words, be analytical, and muster patience. We figure out what we want, what the child wants, and then decide on how to proceed. We don't disregard the child's needs, and we take our own into consideration, too. But as adults, with experience of life, moral sensibilities, an informed perspective, and a long-range plan, we make the tough decisions. No Disney World this year. Milk at dinner each night. Limited television.

The critical question is: What's for me and what's for the baby? These two aren't always mutually exclusive. When you sit at a sick child's bedside, you tend to your child's need for your presence and you feel that you are being a good parent. When you attend a performance at your child's elementary school, you support your child's efforts and you take pleasure in watching your child perform. But when you climb into bed with your sick child to hold and cuddle them, you are first and foremost fulfilling your own need—the need to express your love and protect your child—while misreading the child's real need—the need for perhaps your presence but not your cuddling at that moment. Most children, particularly older ones, do not want to be cuddled when they feel sick. Indeed, a parent's physical closeness can make a sick child feel uncomfortable and can add to his burden. When you sit in the front row of the assembly and clap and cheer uproariously at your child's every action, you are really applauding yourself for having such a talented offspring. Your child is probably embarrassed.

It's increasingly difficult for parents to step back and have some distance from their offspring these days. Some parents just can't tell the difference between their needs and those of their children. They ricochet between viewing their child as the center of the universe and completely forgetting that their child is a *child,* and needs some distance, some supervision, and some restrictions. For one thing, most parents have waited to have children. Some have gone through elaborate and difficult medical procedures to conceive. Others have struggled to adopt. This investment of time, emotion, and money makes it tempting to see the child as something earned, something endlessly special, something "mine," when the precious little one is finally there.

Moreover, many baby-boom and post-baby-boom parents don't really want to be "parents." They are certainly quite conscious of not wanting to be like *their* parents. They don't want to be old. They don't want to slow down. They don't think it's much fun to be the "heavy." Many will even explicitly express this: "I'm much more of a friend to my children than my parents ever were to me."

In the world of our grandparents, becoming a parent was one of the most significant markers of adulthood. You got a job, got married, and then had kids. Then you really, truly were an adult, ready to assume all the responsibilities of same. Many of us can't help but shudder at the thought of ourselves being so uncool. Auto ads reflect this powerfully. They divide the world into two types of cars: sports cars for people who want to forget they're adults, and vans that acknowledge that no one really wants to be seen in a van (how parental and stodgy). Is there any car that an adult with children can drive proudly?

The constant and critical question of parenting is always: Are we meeting our needs or our children's? When we worry if our children like us, we're putting our own needs first. When we try to be pals to our kids, we deprive them of what they really need: the encouragement to develop internal limits, self-control, and behavioral standards.

We're pushed toward the extreme these days—toward constant gratification of our children—because we're encouraged to believe that love means never having to say you're sorry. "Sorry, you can't have more ice cream." "Sorry, you can't watch more TV." "Sorry, it's bedtime." And even, "Sorry, you started your homework too late. You'll have to get up early tomorrow to finish or tell your teacher you didn't finish." It's extremely difficult to resist the notion that love means keeping our children happy.

These attitudes, unwillingness to separate from our children coupled with inability to assume the role of parent, have yielded polarized parenting styles and two varieties of children: "center-of-the-universe babies" and, with a nod to the movie *Austin Powers'* Dr. Evil, "mini-me's." In a contradictory and often confusing fashion, we bounce from enthroning the child, the center-of-the-universe baby, to myopically viewing our child, our "mini-me," as only an extension of our own needs when it suits us.

Let's look at the center-of-the-universe (CU) babies first.

We've seen them, been annoyed by them, and perhaps live with them. I had a pivotal moment years ago that has echoed in my head every time I think of the CU children. I was visiting a friend. Her four-year-old asked for juice. He wanted juice NOW. His mom, who had been interrupted repeatedly by him in the course of our visit, agreed that he could have juice. She took an open carton of orange juice from the fridge and poured him a cup. "NOT THAT JUICE; THIS JUICE!" he hollered, pointing to another carton of orange juice. "No, honey," she explained, "that juice is the same but this carton is already open." "NOT THAT JUICE; THIS JUICE!" he replied. And so she shrugged her shoulders, opened the new carton, and poured THIS JUICE. And so it begins, I thought. Now, this mom may have caved in because she had a friend (me) visiting and wanted to buy some peace. But I don't think so. In any case, the lesson the child received was the same: You are the center of the universe, and if you want THIS JUICE, then THIS JUICE it is.

Parents today exhaust themselves adapting themselves and the world to better fill their child's needs.

Part of this exhaustingly intense focus results in tension at home, sometimes to the point where the mother finds it difficult to be around her child: The child's pain is her pain. If the baby cries, she is frantic. Some mothers find that they can't "be themselves" without getting away, sometimes far away, from their children. This is different from the break that we all need on a regular basis. This is a pathological expression of a mother's inability to separate herself from her child's needs. It might result in parents being more vulnerable to "professionalizing" or "outsourcing" parenting by hiring all kinds of experts to take over child-rearing responsibilities. It's just easier to have the nanny or the tutor or the coach handle it. It's simply too painful to deal with it yourself.

There have been a host of articles recently about SAT coaches. Virtually every article mentions that a good reason to hire an SAT coach is that it removes the emotional content from the process. The child can't scream at the coach when she insists that the child fill out the application forms and submit the required paperwork for various tests. The child can't slam their bedroom door and tell the coach, "You're so all over me all the time," as they might want to do with a nagging parent. While there may well be an argument for detonating potentially explosive teen confrontations, there is something missing in these contractual relationships. Parenting is emotional. Paying is not.

A mother of a thirteen-year-old son recently told me, "I can't bear to do the nagging about homework. It's just too annoying and we're constantly fighting. So I just told him, if he stays on the honor roll, he gets fifty dollars a marking period."

Parents who are raising center-of-the-universe babies often see need where there is no need. They're moms who anticipate too much. Beginning with a dependence on the baby monitor, which we've explored above in the "You Can Manage It All" chapter, they've grown accustomed to being there whenever possible. Partly because they feel guilty about not being there *all the time.* They're hypervigilant, poised to help, to intervene, to encourage. Of course, they're also exhausted.

Many parents identify so strongly with their children—mirror them so powerfully—that they find the nickel-and-dime difficulties inherent in parenting truly overwhelming.

I have a personal solution to this parenting dilemma that I'll share. I call it, with a nod to the campaign discouraging early adolescent sexual relations, "Not me, not now." Every now and again, it should be your parental slogan. Sometimes when they need someone to play with them, to amuse them, to throw the ball, to clap for the song, or to read their homework, you should be able to say, "Not me, not now." Maybe you're finishing a conversation with your husband or an engrossing article in the paper, or maybe you're just chopping onions or taking a bath. Try it. "Not me, not now." It helps.

The flip side of this center-of-the-universe child is the child who begins to develop when the parent is unable to separate adult concerns from children's concerns. These children, these mini-me's, are rushed into adulthood to serve the parents' needs.

I know a father who is totally absorbed in his thirteen-year-old son's nascent interest in girls. He repeats advice he's given his son on "handling" women, and recently told the story of how his son, following Dad's counsel, told a girl that he couldn't come to the phone because he was busy; she'd have to call back later. Aside from what you might think of the quality of this dad's "advice," it's obvious that something's out of whack here. Dad is clearly living through his son, invading his son's discovery of girls and his developing social skills. This father's behavior is a variation on the inappropriate relationship that sometimes develops between a divorced parent and a child. The parent comes to use the child as a confidant, discussing dating issues and financial matters that are best left to adults to sort out. I've heard many parents describe themselves as their child's "best friend"—often a clue to an unhealthy emotional intimacy.

Remember Jessica Dubroff? She was the lovely little seven-year-old girl who was killed in her attempt to become the youngest pilot to fly across the country. It was a tragedy that caused the death of three people—Jessica, her father, and a flight instructor—and a paroxysm of national soul searching about the role of the media in promoting risky behavior and the role of parents in allowing their children to participate in such behavior. While press coverage danced all around the issues, most mothers I know were absolutely unsparing in their disgust with Jessica's parents. How could adults allow and even encourage their own child to risk her life? This was a child who needed extending devices so that her feet could reach the pedals in the plane, and who needed to sit on cushions so that she could see over the controls and out the windshield. There's something deeply disturbing to most adults about the kind of self-absorption evidenced by Jessica's parents, because it mocks the essential bond of trust between parent and child.

I think of young Jessica as an extreme and tragic case of parents losing the boundaries between themselves and their child. Consumed by the dream of a child's success, the parent simply ignores or denies any impulse that says this activity is inappropriate. It's very seductive to erase the boundary between yourself and your child and to assume that your child's success is your success. When the press was flooded with coverage of Jessica Dubroff's story, one mother was hauntingly quoted in a *San Francisco Chronicle* story on mothers, children, and success. She recalled her emotions upon seeing her twin daughters accepting medals for their figure skating. "This was the greatest high you could find," she said. "It's just an amazing feeling. It's like horse racing: That's your horse. That's your prized possession. That's your showpiece. And when they do well, it's easy for a parent's need for recognition, for filling unfulfilled dreams, to surface . . . We all became junkies for our kids' success."

Jessica Dubroff's mother so identified with her that she began to think like a seven-year-old. Two days before Jessica took off, her mother, Lisa Blair Hathaway, was asked if the weather might delay her flight east. Her response was, "The weather will move for her. It is not luck. Jessica knows that. It is the power of her being. There is something about Jessica that things move for her. She is just a wonderful person." Jessica Dubroff was never allowed to live in a real world of childhood. As she explained to the *Chronicle* when asked about whether her child might be frightened about flying a plane by herself, "We don't use an emotional-thinking language, so we don't use the words 'scared,' 'fear,' 'sadness,' 'happy.' " Hathaway remarked, "I'm not nervous in any way, because Jessica is a great aviator. I see it in her body and soul, and there is no way I would ruin that for her by being nervous."

Dr. Roy Meadow, an English pediatrician, has described the vicarious celebrity a parent receives in these situations as Achievement by Proxy Syndrome. Meadow described ABPS in 1997 as a variation on Munchausen Syndrome by Proxy, in which intelligent and apparently caring mothers induce illness and even death in their children to gain attention for themselves.

Sadly, this is an extreme example of overidentification with a child. But many parents today regularly ignore risks and dangers that their children endure in a quest for a measure of success that usually is the parent's, not the child's, goal. For example, the increase in sports injuries among young people is astronomical. The entire specialty of pediatric sports medicine owes its existence to our allowing our children to "overdo" it with sports. Broken bones, torn ligaments, and more serious injuries have become routine. At the middle- and high school levels, children of various sizes, fitness, and skill levels may be paired in competitions. This alone can increase risk of an injury. And young athletes are more susceptible to injury because their bones, muscles, tendons, and ligaments are still growing. I know of one mother of an eighth-grade son who was annoyed at the high school football coach who was encouraging her son to work with the team the summer before high school. "Yes, he's a good athlete and large for his age, but he is still thirteen, and I don't want him in violent contact with boys four years older." This wise mom is the exception. Other friends of hers, she reported, were thrilled that the coach was interested in their sons.

There is lots of evidence of our difficulty in separating our children's needs from our own both in the news and in the culture. JonBenet Ramsey, age six, was the young beauty pageant winner who was found strangled in her Boulder, Colorado, home—a murder that is still unsolved. Her mother, Patricia Ramsey, a former Miss West Virginia, is reported to have insisted that she and her daughter shared the desire to compete in beauty contests.

Everything from designer fashions for toddlers to bike buggies to ski snugglies and jogging strollers signal an inability to distinguish between what's right and appropriate for a child and what is simply a convenience or an ego-boost for a parent.

Take those jogging strollers. You've seen them. They have a single wheel in front and two wheels in back, and they allow parents to keep up with their fitness goals. The child is strapped into the device, and the parent is soon back doing five miles before breakfast. Just like before baby. Certainly these strollers serve parents' needs, and they make us feel very efficient because we're getting in shape and the baby is with us, but what about the child's experience? Baby and toddler speed is slow. You know how a toddler will pick up a pebble and examine it thoroughly and completely? That's how slow the toddler world is. In the jogging stroller they're whizzing by at a fantastic rate speed, eyes glazed, unable to focus on anything. Perhaps some small children are even frightened by the experience.

Bike buggies allow you to pull your child along behind you

while you ride your bike. On the road it can be dangerous; on bike trails it's probably just uncomfortable. Ski snugglies, I believe, are dangerous as well as uncomfortable. I recently saw a man ski down an intermediate slope with an infant in a backpack on his back. When another skier cut him off—a near-miss that could have had a disastrous outcome for the infant—the father was enraged. "Can't you see I have an infant on my back?" he yelled with righteous indignation.

Parents justify such activities by convincing themselves that it's good for the child to get out in the fresh air. It's quite obvious that they do it because they want to jog or ski. Perhaps some children really do enjoy the stimulation. What's clear is that most children can get used to just about anything, and they're happy if you're happy. But it can be a mistake to ignore the child's genuine needs and safety.

The issue of "whom it's for" becomes most difficult, complicated, and painful when it comes to mothers working. There is no easy answer to this dilemma, but it's important to be honest about how our children cope with our absence. A study has just been published regarding the effects of day care on children, concluding that the effects are more negative than we previously thought. While there may be other variables, it is clear that our children do miss us and need us.

A mother in an article in *The Wall Street Journal* explains the benefits for her children of her and her spouse's demanding careers: "I think kids need some distance from their parents to grow. It's really important for kids to make mistakes, accept their mistakes, and learn from them. I think a real plus of my working is that you children are learning to be self-sufficient and feel good about the decisions you make." She goes on to explain that she's "made a big point of putting the kids first in terms of seeing that they're not being sacrificed because of our careers."

This is a refrain you've no doubt heard before. But it's interesting to hear the children's response: "Sometimes we want to talk to her when we come home from school, and we get kind of annoyed that she's on the phone. Also, even though she works pretty close, it's kind of hard for her to come home. If we were sick or something, she could pick us up, but it would be hard."

There's no simple answer here, but it helps to tell the truth. Do these children feel that they're being put first in their parents' lives? I doubt it. They might feel better about things if their parents, particularly their mother, explained that she loved to work, found it satisfying and engrossing, and hoped that when they grew up, they would find something to do that would give them as much pleasure. In the meantime, she might work harder to listen to their concerns about her absence. Because from their standpoint as children viewing an adult world, the emperor has no clothes: Mom and Dad say the arrangement is good and that everyone is happy, but deep in the children's hearts there may be another story.

Lisa Belkin of the *New York Times* had a recent struggle with this dichotomy between what's real and what's not in relation to children and the world of work. In her regular column, "Life's Work," she wrestled with the dilemma posed by Take Our Daughters to Work Day. How, she wondered, do we teach our children about work? If we teach them that work is fun and fulfilling, how do we explain how irritable and exhausted we are at the end of the day? And if we teach them that work is hard and difficult, and that we'd really rather be reading bedtime stories to them but we can't because we need to pay the rent, then are we teaching them to dread the rest of their lives when they'll be working each day? But here's a point to consider: It's not always our responsibility to explain the world to them as we see it. Much as we care and much as we want them to see things our way, in the end, we can't. Sometimes we have to forget about the "take-home" message. Relax a bit. We don't really have to explain the whole world to our children. We can put down the mirror. It's not really our responsibility. They'll surely figure at least some of it out on their own.

Almost Perfect

We push our children because they're almost there, they're almost perfect. They're great kids; smart, funny, lively. But with just a bit of a nudge, a bit of encouragement, a little bit extra . . . Well, it just might make all the difference.

In my hospital practice I work with families who have been dealt a difficult hand. Their children are sick or injured. They are struggling to recover and lead as full a life as possible. Whether their children have suffered a gunshot wound, a disabling chronic condition like cerebral palsy, or a traumatic brain injury, the parents must reassess their children's lives in ways that most parents will, fortunately, never face. For these parents the world has shifted, and they see their children, on the whole, differently from other parents.

In my private practice, I work with parents whose children are suffering from different, less apparent, though often no less devastating, problems. They may be learning disabled. They may be anxious or suffer from obsessive-compulsive disorder or childhood depression. These families, in many cases, are adjusting very slowly to the idea that their child has a disability—usually an emotional disability—of some kind. Sometimes these families never face the fact that their children may not become the wishful fantasy of what they held dear when their child was an infant. Sometimes their very clinging to that promise is what has brought the child to me in the first place.

If your child is disabled, born with a birth defect, or suffers a disfiguring accident, you are positioned to recognize more clearly what's possible and what's not for your child. For your mental health as well as your child's, you revise your expectations to fit what is possible. Of course, every parent has hopes and dreams for their child. But a parent who has been forced to reassess their child's possibilities because of an illness or injury has usually also found that their "narcissistic edge"—the part of parenting that can push beyond reason—is softened. This is generally a positive development.

But if your child is an A student in a good school system, a good soccer player with a flair for chess, or perhaps a lacrosse player with a flair for the trumpet, who knows? The sky's the limit. You, the parent, are pushed by possibility. It's not the plain, book-wormish tenth-grade girl who's going to be encouraged by parents and friends to go for the prom queen throne. It's the pretty, social one who's just over 127 pounds who would look so fabulous if she just slimmed down a bit. This is the girl who's *almost perfect,* who's available to be pushed. This is also the girl who's the candidate to develop anorexia nervosa.

It is the combination of all the hype that propels us ("Be all that you can be!" "Just Do It!") plus the loving, bright child who wants more than anything to please us that pushes us to the edge of this treacherous cliff. "You could be so great at piano if we got you a better teacher and you really gave it your all." "The coach told me you'd make varsity for sure if you worked over the summer and maybe did some serious weight training."

The parental impulse today is to become a coach, a cheering section. But the focus far too often is on what *could* be, not what is. Kids aren't encouraged to focus on what they've accomplished, but rather on what they *could* accomplish if only . . . Children who want to please their parents—and this includes almost all children—and who are motivated by praise and attention, become almost blinded by their parents' enthusiasm for excellence. Frequently they foreclose on any conflicting feelings they may have. "I'm not that wild about tennis," they may say, "but my parents just love that I'm playing. They're even talking about getting a court put in." These children nail down the coffin on their ambivalence and throw themselves full force into the fray.

It's important for parents to understand that there is a difference between hope and denial. Parents must be filled with hope for their children. Hope (I hope Mary makes the team—I hope the test results come back negative) is critical. It empowers people and supports them through loss and through challenging times. But denial (There's no doubt you're the best player at the tryouts. Certainly he's not depressed; he's just been tired.) can be destructive. It's a blind spot that compromises accurate assessments, impairs future planning, and distances people from one another.

When you live in the land of opportunity, and the tradition is that each generation climbs a rung higher in the social and economic strata than their parents, all of the things you don't do, or, more important, your children don't do, become deficiencies.

The temptation to push your almost-perfect kid to the top

of the heap is even harder to resist these days. There are so many things you can do to help, and many of these things are encouraged by our culture. I recently read about an infant toy called "The Babbler." It is one of the many new high-tech infant toys containing computer chips that promise to improve your child. The Babbler is a large stuffed circle with a half-moon face and a teething ring. When the baby manipulates it, rolls on it, or bites it, it emits whisper sounds from several languages. Who could resist? The Babbler is supposedly based on the latest research on language development in children. Many studies have demonstrated that most children can learn foreign languages at very early ages, and they learn even more readily the younger they are. Parents have become eager to expose their babies to foreign languages before the age of three. Research has also shown that infants can discriminate among phonemes (the tiniest sound bites of words) from foreign languages when they are only a few months old. The Babbler exploits the notion that if you expose an infant to a larger range of phonemes, he or she will be better prepared to learn a foreign language at a very early age. The seed will have been sown. The Babbler is the infant preamble to the toddler "Little Linguist," an interactive computer toy that a child can use to learn to speak a foreign language. Certainly The Babbler or the Little Linguist will harm nothing but your pocketbook. The difficulty is that the very existence of such toys (which after all are sold to make money, not to educate your child) begins the process wherein a parent believes they can and should "improve" their baby.

It's very hard to resist that urge to "cover all bases" as far as your child is concerned, to do everything within your power to move them one step closer to perfect.

Of course The Babbler is just one of countless devices from "lap ware" computer programs for toddlers to SAT prep courses that help to prune and groom our children's intellectual achievement. The implicit message of these products, courses, and professionals is that a child needs perfecting, and that it's not so difficult to accomplish if you, the parent, have the will, the stamina, and the money to move your child from good to great.

It's not only intellectual and athletic benchmarking that seems to need improving these days. Children's physical appearance is now also considered "improvable." Encouraged by the same hypes already discussed in the "Media Life Equals Real Life" and "Everybody's Doing It!" chapters, parents more and more readily accept the logic of altering a child's appearance.

Surely you've noticed that very few children reach high school without braces on their teeth. Years ago, for both economic and cultural reasons, a parent consulted an orthodontist when a child had markedly crooked teeth. Now any child with the slightest abnormality will be encouraged to correct it. It's also relatively easy and acceptable to get a child's teeth whitened, bonded, or capped.

While we've all come to accept dental improvements as expected and absolutely routine (indeed, the parent who failed to straighten a child's crooked teeth would be considered neglectful), the potential for cosmetic improvement is now beginning to reach the point where ethical decisions must be made about its appropriateness.

Plastic surgery has become increasingly common among young people. While rhinoplasty, or the nose job, has been around for a long time, it's now more acceptable than ever before for teenagers to undergo chin implants, liposuction, and even breast augmentation. America's love affair with relentless improvement is evident in the statistics published by the American Society for Aesthetic Plastic Surgery. Cosmetic surgery has increased in popularity over the years, with a 173 percent increase in procedures between 1997 and 2000. And while it may be reassuring to read that the rate of teenage plastic surgery has remained stable (around 3 percent), that is really another way of saying that teenage cosmetic surgery has paralleled the steep rise in surgery in the adult population.

Almost any surgeon will tell you, "There is no such thing as minor surgery." By that they mean that general anesthesia is a risk, and postoperative complications are a real and serious, albeit unlikely, possibility for any kind of surgery, no matter how "minor."

The American Academy of Facial Plastic and Reconstructive Surgery has come out against breast augmentation for anyone under age eighteen. Despite this position, the high school senior who receives longed-for breast augmentation as a graduation present is not a rarity. And liposuction among teens now accounts for approximately 2 percent of the total liposuction performed in the United States.

Adolescence is a time when youngsters frequently become preoccupied with a particular part of their body. They hate their hair, their eyes, their noses. Their breasts are too small, their tummies too big, their ankles too wide. We're all well aware of how our culture fans these flames of discontent. I had a young female patient with severe social anxiety. She was seventeen when I first met her and she had already had a nose job. She was still dissatisfied with the result and believed with all her heart that if only her nose were smaller, she would fit in, have friends, and life would be far better. No surgery, of course, would solve her difficulties, but when the possibility of surgery exists, it's hard for young people to understand that a physical feature may not be the cause of their problems.

Sometimes these enhancements have an ironic result: In

some cases, the better a child looks, the worse he or she feels. Certainly there are many cases where surgery or cosmetic enhancement of some kind has improved a youngster's life or boosted their confidence. But there are also many cases where a cosmetic procedure has been an effort to "gild the lily" and has been promoted and encouraged primarily by a parent. While few would argue against orthodontic work that corrects a poor bite or gap-toothed smile, what argument can one make for a breast augmentation for a seventeen-year-old girl? Think back for just a moment to some of the identities you tried on during adolescence, and imagine what it would be like if you had to live with them forever.

The obvious implicit message when a parent agrees to cosmetic improvement is "you're not good enough the way you are." While I surely wouldn't dissuade anyone from any kind of cosmetic surgery that they felt would truly improve their life, it's critical that these procedures should be performed, in most cases, on adults with a realistic assessment of how the procedure will affect their life, not on a child or adolescent who is in the difficult process of forming a complete sense of self.

This drive to perfect our children doesn't only affect the way we mold and prune their physical and academic performance. In our intense focus on their résumés, we're actually changing the way we perceive our children. As our expectations for our children ratchet up, we increasingly limit the behaviors that we consider normal. I remember a neighbor when I was a child who had six children. Her second-youngest, who was perhaps her wildest in a wild bunch, was never referred to without rolled eyes, a shake of the head, and an affectionate "that nut . . . she'll be the end of me." Few parents today would casually and routinely refer to one of their kids this way. I don't mean to applaud the Great Santini approach to child-rearing. I'm simply pointing out that in years past there was perhaps a healthier acceptance of a broader range of childhood behaviors. There was also less onerous pressure on parents to take full responsibility for their children's behavioral idiosyncrasies.

Our job description of childhood has become extremely narrow. As we've limited the range of behaviors that we consider acceptable, we have embraced cosmetic psychopharmacology— the use of medications to alter the nonpathological behavior of children. It's another weapon in the arsenal we can use to bring our children a smidge closer to perfect. A drug can bridge the gap between our children as good and our children as almost perfect.

It's hard for many parents to accept a near miss. Why settle for a 650 on the SAT when an intensive prep course and maybe even a stimulant will boost the grade? Why sacrifice a high class ranking because a hockey tournament makes it tough to finish a paper? It is extremely tempting for some parents to give an extra dose of medication this one time so their child will still be in the running.

A huge increase in medication for Attention Deficit Hyperactivity Disorder (ADHD) has occurred since 1990. Estimates of the total number of American children diagnosed with ADHD who are being medicated doubled from 750,000 children in 1989 to 1.5 million in 1995. Some researchers have also found a positive correlation between increased medication use and higher socioeconomic class.

Likewise the number of children and adolescents receiving drug therapy for anxiety and depression has increased. While it is impossible to come up with an accurate number, a *Time* magazine article in May 1999 estimated that 500,000 to 1 million antidepressant prescriptions are written each year for children and adolescents. And the number is growing. Depression has been on the rise with each decade since the turn of the last century. Currently, an estimated 1 percent of preschoolers, 2 percent of school-age children, and 5 percent of adolescents experience clinical depression. This population of depressed kids is made up in part by children who are under increasing amounts of pressure to perform, to be productive and successful.

Prozac has become a popular drug for several reasons. The selective serotonin reuptake inhibitors (SSRIs), of which Prozac is the prototype, are not only effective treatments for many forms of depression and anxiety, but they also have relatively mild side effects. They are so well tolerated in fact that one internist in Manhattan remarked, "All my patients in their thirties, who don't seem that depressed, ask me for Prozac. It's the elderly ones, who I am really worried about and want to prescribe it to. They refuse to even try it." Of course, elderly people represent a generation unaccustomed to taking drugs for emotional problems. Indeed, many elderly people who survived the Depression and a world war are almost scornful of the notion of relying on medication. While they perhaps represent an unhealthy extreme, it's interesting to note how readily younger people will use a medication to improve the way they feel.

An estimated 35 million people were taking Prozac in 1999. In his book, *Listening to Prozac,* Dr. Peter Kramer eloquently frames the dilemma of treating maladaptive character traits with Prozac. I wonder if we are doing a similar intervention with some of our "almost perfect" children. Despite recent attention to much-needed research in the area of child psychopharmacology, this is for the most part uncharted territory. Whenever I write a prescription for a child or teenager I am concerned not just about the possible adverse side effects, but also the unknowns. What about the subtle changes impacting the child's personality development? Are they all for the good? Do we even know what they are?

In a fascinating article in *The New Yorker,* Jerome Groopman reports on personality and behaviors, particularly behavioral disorders, and their relationship with the environment. He realized that many prominent scientists demonstrated some traits associated with clinical disorders. One psychologist he interviewed, Jane Holmes Bernstein, the director of the neuropsychology program at Boston's Children's Hospital, found herself working with a child, referred to her because of various learning disorders. Dr. Bernstein, who had administered the full battery of neuropsychiatric tests to herself, discovered that the referred child tested exactly as she herself had tested. She asked herself rhetorically why she was on her side of the desk, recognizing that, "In my environment, I function at a high level, where it plays out adaptively." The child, of course, in a school setting, forced to be a generalist, has trouble adapting. What's the point? Well, though I work with children who require medication to function in their everyday lives, and though I routinely prescribe medication for children and believe that it allows them to lead less burdensome lives, I also recognize that using medication as a kind of homogenization to mold children after a generally adapted standard of behavior is not useful. As Dr. Bernstein says, "Left to itself, the human animal accepts a wide range of behavior." Children need a parent who can modify their expectations and guide them to develop coping skills, before considering altering their worlds through medication.

Unfortunately, whether we maneuver our almost-there children closer to perfect via medication, surgery, coaching, or just the pressure of our expectations, one of the results is a persistent undermining of their competence and confidence. Changing their world via external means is not empowering. While we might all feel the impulse to nudge our child toward an A, the challenge is to take the longer view and step back a bit. When a child has his own idea of what he wants to change, conceptualizes how he'll achieve this, manages to accomplish it, and enjoys his success, that is the pattern that yields success and happiness. Our almost-perfect child, left to his own devices, secure in our love and support, may be far closer to perfection than we can perceive.

PART II

The Fallout of Push Parenting

The Pushed-Apart Family

A family is a system and a process. It consists of one or two adults and one or more children. Beyond those basics, every family is its own country. It creates, implicitly, its own constitution, its own customs, its own food, and its own history. For most of us, establishing and living within our families is simultaneously the most demanding and challenging, creative and satisfying part of our lives.

The largest portion of a family's culture takes form without much conscious thought. A Greek family may relish the baklava recipe that Yiayia makes. The family in Colorado might all be avid skiers. In addition to what geography and ethnic heritage dictate, we make choices about many aspects of our families' lives. How many children do we want? Are we strict or permissive? How do we handle money? Is our house neat as a pin or a bit of a shambles?

Healthy families usually have a system of checks and balances: Mom is exhausted so Dad makes dinner or at least orders takeout. Dad gets overheated about a broken window, Mom pours oil on the waters and reestablishes peace. Sometimes one or the other parent seems superfluous, dare we say outright annoying. But we often need that fresh perspective to pull us from the brink. Moms have been known to get so immersed in the overheated, hothouse life with small children, tons of plastic figures, and the scent of Play-Doh that they veer out of control. I can recall the story of a mom sitting stupefied in the midst of chaos at 6 P.M. while the TV blared with a violent wrestling program. She vacantly mouth-breathed while her three sons pummeled one another. Until, that is, Dad arrived home, strode purposefully to the TV, switched it off, and commented, "I don't think we'll encourage this." Sometimes one or the other parent needs that figurative slap in the face that restores reason. In many families, Mom serves as the emotional chiropractor, making adjustments to the family dynamic (Dad hasn't been spending enough time with Suzie; Billy has been withdrawn because his best friend is moving away), while Dad is the mechanic ("If you want to improve your jump shot, Mandy, you're just going to have to practice"). Single-parent families have to find their reference points from friends or family members who can reassure them that it's not a complete disaster if their three-year-old daughter refuses to eat vegetables or their nine-year-old son didn't make the traveling soccer team. Every family needs help in establishing a perspective, whether that help comes from a spouse, a grandparent, a friend, or a teacher.

When the balance of a family is disrupted, or when the perspective is lost, everyone feels it. I've seen striking similarities between families enduring the emotional trial of a sick child and families, all too common today, who have sacrificed family life to the elusive goal of the children's "achievement." Whether it's the family that's decided to take their daughter's skill at figure skating and "go with it" until practices and travel dominate all family decisions, or the family that allows a plethora of activities, lessons, and pursuits to dictate the family schedule, many of today's children are living in a "pushed-apart" family—one that's abandoned a balanced system of emotional and practical considerations that are necessary to keep families healthy. Most members of a pushed-apart family suffer in immediate as well as far-reaching ways.

I must keep in mind the importance of family balance when I'm working with families who have a sick or injured child. Family anxiety levels are high, when the focus of their world shifts to the sick child. Siblings can become silent patients: They are often ignored because they're not the "identified patient," the really sick one. In these crisis situations, siblings often suffer enormously. Consumed with worry about their sick brother or sister, they also pick up on their parents' stress and anxiety. Frequently, they have an undercurrent of guilt that grows out of the ambivalence typical of any sibling relationship. (How many times did they tell their brother to just "drop dead"?)

Siblings of sick children also must cope with specific concrete changes in their family life. Their meals are often disrupted, routines evaporate. Some children act out when forced to cope with these changes. Others, whose behavior during a crisis is just too good to be true, are often actually extremely anxious, but intuit that there's no room in their life for them to react to the upheaval. This doesn't make it any less painful for them.

"Unidentified patient" siblings usually endure these various fears, disruptions, and anxieties alone because their parents are too preoccupied with the sick child and their own fears and worries. So siblings of a sick child have lots to worry about, and they're getting less parenting to help diffuse that worry.

A pushed-apart family, as opposed to a family with a sick child, loses its balance insidiously over a period of time. Neither the moment of a diagnosis nor the aftermath of an accident commences the shift; it's a more drawn-out process. Perhaps Dad identifies with little Sam's interest in hockey. His son is an eager pupil, so Dad invests in some valuable equipment, gets him started on a peewee team, and hires a coach to work with Sam a few mornings a week. Games become family affairs and Sam's sister soon finds that her Saturday mornings are spent doing homework at the rink, or visiting over at a friend's house so she won't be "bored" during practice. Relaxed weekend breakfasts become a memory as free time becomes "ice time." Within a few years, Dad is beginning to think about college scholarships for Sam (never mind that hockey scholarships are as rare as Montreal Canadiens' original teeth). Hockey has taken over the family: Vacations are devoted to tournament travel, and family friendships and social interactions revolve around hockey. Even schoolwork becomes secondary, not explicitly—most parents give at least lip service to the importance of good grades—but implicitly. Tests, term papers, and special projects are never allowed to interfere with practice or game time. Dad begins to brag that Sam can practically do his math while he skates, and that staying up till midnight to finish a paper doesn't faze him a bit.

Mom and Sis, and even Dad, have become satellites of Sam and his hockey.

With some families, the scenario differs in its emphasis.

Rather than one child with an identified ability becoming the focus, all the children are pushed. In these situations, the ante is upped because simple time constraints dictate that when you pile tutors and coaches and lessons and practices and home-work onto the plate, family life disappears. Moreover, in most ultrabusy, competitive families, it soon becomes apparent that one or two children have greater ability or potential than the others. The balance and focus of the family shifts as the parents push the child with the potential or the temperament to re-spond to pushing. The other children become also-rans. Like children in a family facing illness, they become the silent pa-tients, and for the same reasons. They either act out or suffer silently, living with hurt, anger, and anxiety.

Many parents defend their focus on sports or other compet-itive activities, cherishing the notion that their children "really thrive on it," or that "it's good training for real life." One star-tling yet all too common justification for these activities' dom-inance in their children's lives is that these demands "teach them to manage their time." To me, this approach is akin to putting a child on a bed of hot coals with the goal of teaching him to walk faster.

Some aspects of our everyday life that push our families apart are very hard to control or manage. Work, for example, seems to be the most confounding issue for today's families. These days, whether the economy is good or bad, work seems to drain off more and more time for people who are employed. Partly because so many companies have downsized and reduced staff, jobs that two people (or even more) used to handle easily are now juggled by one harried worker. More and more people work late, go in early, and commute long distances to fulfill work obligations.

In terms of a home life with children, perhaps the most difficult part of work's demands is that technology has made us more and more available to work more and more. We can check our e-mails even on the beach, to say nothing of on a Sunday morning. If it were impossible to be in touch with colleagues and clients, we wouldn't even think about it. But when we know that in just five seconds we can log on and check to see if we've heard about that crucial deal, we become preoccupied. We're used to multitasking; it's difficult to turn off this harried, preoccupied mentality when we get home.

What is the pushed-apart family missing? Primarily, what they're missing is time together—something that they'll never have an opportunity to recapture. One study reported that in the past twelve years, household conversations have decreased one hundred percent!—an absolutely stunning figure, even allowing for a wide margin of error. One of the most critical components to reading readiness and success is providing a child with a language-rich environment. What a shame that families, while spending a small fortune on tutors and private schools, are no longer talking!

We all know that family dinners are disappearing as parents sacrifice the restorative pleasure of eating together, and their children's nutrition, to fast food en route in the van. Children between the ages of nine and fourteen who have regular dinners with their families have proven to have more healthful dietary patterns, which include consuming more fruits and vegetables, less saturated fat, fewer fried foods and sodas, and more vitamins and other micronutrients. (These results, by the way, held true after statistical controls for household income, maternal employment, body mass index, physical activity, and other factors were considered.) But many of us are too tired, too stressed, and too short of time to focus on putting together a real meal, even if the family is in one place long enough to eat it together.

In the same twelve years that we've seen a stunning decline in family conversation, we've seen a doubling of children's structured sports time and a fivefold increase in the amount of time that children spend in passive, spectator leisure (going to the movies, playing video games, using computers), and that figure doesn't even include television time. In the 1970s, a *Wall Street Journal* article reported teenagers could play two or three sports in high school. The hockey season then used to be three or four months a year. Now a hockey season can run fifty weeks. Practices are more frequent, and players can be benched for not showing up at practice. Children have precious little free time and half the unstructured outdoor playtime that they had just over ten years ago. A University of Michigan study done in 1998 found that free time for children under age thirteen has fallen 16 percent in a single generation—to 51 from 63 hours a week.

The quest for perfection in all child-related activities puts parents in the backseat. They're no longer setting priorities according to their own goals for the family and for their lives together. Because they are pressured from every direction to get their kids to "be the best that they can be," parents find that it's harder and harder to seize control of their family lives. As "goals" become increasingly important (making the team, getting terrific SAT scores, building the résumé), daily life recedes into the dull background. Having dinner together, watching a movie, going to religious services, simply being at home, become less important than being tutored in a language or getting ice time or traveling to distant towns to compete in various sports.

It's critical to know your child. Some children truly thrive on the opportunity to compete or to pursue a particular interest. Others just want to be at home. But even children who thrive on activity need the restorative balance, peace, and support of a family life.

A family is a system. When all the towels land on one side of the washer, it sounds like a freight train and walks across the floor. It's still spinning but it's working under protest. When one member of a family takes on an outsize role, unless it's temporary or due to something—illness, injury, work demands—outside the family's ability to control, the family will continue on, but it's not working efficiently and serving all members as it should.

It's all about balance. The toll the unbalanced family takes on children is real and soon apparent. They become anxious and stressed. While most parents are eager to embrace the notion of "bonding" at the instant of birth, many of these same parents ignore the toll that parental absence takes on older children. Perhaps it's because "studies" haven't emphasized this, or perhaps it's because the pressure to "achieve" takes precedence over vague notions of children's emotional health. But children are suffering. In a 2000 national poll taken by the Global Strategy Group, 21 percent of teens rated "not having enough time together with parents" as their top concern. And that's just the percentage who could recognize this lack and articulate it. No doubt it underestimates of the number of teens who *need* their parents around more. Another study of younger children by the Institute for Youth Development in Washington, D.C., found in focus groups with 429 children ages eleven to fourteen that they want more of a sense of connectedness with parents and more time doing simple things together.

The psychological principle at work here is "attachment" and connection and, as I mentioned, we seem ready to consider this issue with infants and babies, who actually demand attention by crying. Older children rarely give any direct indication that they are missing *you.* But the same concepts of attachment still apply: A child needs attention from a parent who tolerates, who is patient, affectionate, and reassuring, yet autonomous enough to set limits. As a *Wall Street Journal* "Work & Family" column recently stated in a headline: "Children Want Parents to Stop Making Plans and Start Hanging Out." I am not suggesting that parents take up skateboarding or work on their videogame response time, but I am saying that time "doing nothing" is something—something important.

Children aren't the only ones to suffer from a pushed-apart family locked into overdrive. Parents, overburdened and pressured by work and a rigorous schedule, begin to suffer from the stress of trying to keep all the balls in the air. They can't afford to be patient when their two-year-old dawdles about getting dressed. They must be at soccer in ten minutes! If the eight-year-old wants to skip practice, they're dismayed. It's not unreasonable for a third grader to want to go to a sleepover, but the coach won't tolerate skipping practices and a big game is coming up. They'll be benched if they don't practice. Often parents feel conflicted in these situations. On the one hand, they want their child to be able to be involved in a variety of activities, particularly social events that aren't routine occasions. On the other hand, they rationalize that the child must learn the hard facts of life: If you want something, you have to work for it.

And there's also the resentment factor. After all, Mom and Dad are sacrificing a lot to further the gymnastics or violin, and they're doing it "for your own good." They're missing movies and dinners out and quiet, relaxing evenings at home. Often they have to work longer hours to meet the heavy financial burden of achievement. They know they can't quite expect a ten-year-old to be grateful, but they can expect a little cooperation. Children pick up on their parents' buried resentment and exasperation. At this point, most simply swallow any ambivalence about performing because they sense that there's just too much at stake. Many children get to the point where they feel they and their parents have invested so much in time, money, and dreams of success that they simply can't afford to quit.

And what about *us?* How is our marriage holding up? Too often when the focus is entirely on the child's life, the marriage suffers. There's just no time to be a couple, and it's so often easier to worry about soccer sign-up, arranging for tutors, and divvying up the weekend driving than to worry about the rough spots inevitable in every marriage. The "job" of the marriage becomes perfecting the child. In addition to the distraction factor that push parenting creates, there's also the disappointment and resentment factor. What if the child loses the championship? Doesn't make the team? Doesn't get into the legacy school? Then if that was the focus of the family, the marriage, what's the point? Said one high school freshman who was not invited to return to her music camp the following summer because her talent was deemed "inadequate," a crushing blow to her eager parents, "They are so angry and disappointed, they aren't even speaking to each other."

So here you have a not atypical American family: pushed apart emotionally and physically by the competitive demands of a high-pressure culture.

We usually don't see these changes in our families happening, and we don't even know what we're missing. Many families rarely experience quiet, spontaneous times. They never consider an alternative. They feel that "work hard, play hard" is a cultural imperative.

One sure thing: You can't count on your child to pull the plug. You, the parent, have to choose to deescalate. For many of us, it's far more unsettling to pause than simply to keep going.

The Entitled, High-Maintenance Child

I don't really enjoy shopping for clothes. I'm always in a hurry; I always should be somewhere else. But one day, when I could put it off no longer, I ran into Banana Republic to buy some jeans. I grabbed a few pair in my size and ran into the dressing room. They were all too big. I hadn't lost weight, so I was perplexed. It took me two more trips to the dressing room before I found jeans that fit. As I paid for them, I asked the cashier about the odd sizing. "Oh," she explained, "that's our 'vanity sizing.'"

A lightbulb went on over my head: "vanity sizing"! We are all being vanity sized. Everyone is working very hard behind the scenes to make us feel good about ourselves. Indeed, vanity sizing has migrated from the dressing room to the classroom to the home. Even our children are being "vanity sized": the B's magically turned to A's. The "goods" turned to "greats," and the mere participants became champions.

Perhaps your child has a room cluttered with trophies and ribbons. My own son has a supersize trophy that could use a room of its own. He got it for showing up, some of the time, at a soccer clinic. A five-year-old girl I know was given someone else's award at a gymnastics competition. She never bothered to make the exchange for the correct award. She had so many awards cluttering her room, it just didn't seem to matter. While certainly all children are, in their parents' eyes, award winners, official recognition of this status, on the playground, in the classroom, and on the home front has given us a generation filled with children who are poorly equipped to cope with the reality that awaits them beyond the land of trophies and "super!" stickers.

Vanity sizing has operated to our children's particular disadvantage in the classroom, where parents and teachers have sometimes lost sight of actual learning in favor of feeling. As one mother in a suburban New York school complained, "There doesn't really seem to be anyone at the school who really *loves* my child." In *The Feel-Good Curriculum: The Dumbing Down of America's Kids in the Name of Self-Esteem,* Maureen Stout makes a powerful argument against the self-esteem movement. As she says, one of the reasons the public school is constantly under fire "is that the public can rarely agree on just what education should be and thus schools are constantly trying to balance conflicting political, social, and educational interests. But what is clear is that [until recently] the cultivation of self-esteem was never an overriding interest and was only considered (if it was considered at all) a consequence of achievement, hard work, and responsibility. Only recently in the history of American schooling has self-esteem become the primary goal of education."

Stout goes on to accuse professors of education of promoting the classroom as a place in which children are insulated from the outside world and emotionally, as opposed to intellectually, nourished. As she says, "Schools are no longer for learning essential skills or acquiring knowledge, but for cultivating what Daniel Goleman calls 'emotional intelligence': the ability to get along with others, understand one's feelings and one's emotional hang-ups, and generally figure out how to deal with others effectively."

Her position is controversial, and it does seem that the pendulum is swinging the other way with a recent emphasis on "outcome-based" education that looks to results. But the pervasive concern with self-esteem, in the classroom, on the playing field and, most of all, at home, has had its effect. After all, is it really to a child's advantage to have a teacher say to a student who's given an incorrect answer, "That's the right answer to another question"?

Vanity sizing in and of itself is not terrible. It's a simple ploy, a mild trick to fool people into feeling good. It's like calibrating the bathroom scale at a bit under zero, or setting our watches a few minutes fast so we're always "early." But it's a good example of the kind of parenting technique that ultimately backfires and encourages attitudes like "entitlement" that render our children high maintenance. These are children who expect the world to come to them; who feel that they deserve the best, who believe that they are "entitled" to the best life has to offer. They often have difficulty making good moral choices and empathizing with others. Vanity sizing doesn't cause high maintenance; it's only one factor common to parenting today that encourages this trend. And it seems to encapsulate mistaken notions of what children want and need from their parents.

It all started with progressive parenting in the sixties with Dr. Spock at the helm. Strict rules, formal feeding schedules, and black-and-white child-rearing dogmas—boys don't play with dolls, children must be in bed by 8 P.M.—were revised. Parents were no longer willing to exert their power simply by force of will coupled with might. Parenting became less dogmatic and more cooperative. Many of these changes were for the better, and many parents and children enjoyed a new intimacy and warmth based on mutual respect and understanding. But, as seems inevitable in cultural swings, many parents were swept unthinkingly into fashionable parenting practices that seemed to ignore common sense.

For example, it became fashionable to give children choices, to "empower" them. A pre-schooler can be a candidate for this parenting technique. "Would you rather walk to the car or would you like me to carry you?" "Would you like to wear your jeans or your sweatpants?" There are many occasions when giving a child a choice is a sensible approach. And again, it's not much of a choice: You *are* getting in the car. You *are* putting on pants. But the simple technique that's averted many a temper tantrum has too often become perverted. Notice that in the examples given, the parent has offered two choices that are appropriate and acceptable. It is not an open-ended choice, but one that has simply narrowed the possibilities.

Today many parents pretend that their children are able and competent to choose. And not simply one thing versus another. It's too easy to fall into the trap of giving them open-ended choices that are sometimes entirely inappropriate to their maturity and sophistication. Parents and teachers alike are developing chronic spinal conditions as they bend over backward to nuture children's self-esteem by encouraging them to participate in making choices. Which crayon would you like to use? Which restaurant should we eat at? Which dress should Mom wear? What kind of car, appliance, or computer should we buy? We've been led to believe that allowing them to choose empowers them.

In fact, a child making an open-ended choice—a choice inappropriate to their age, wisdom, and maturity—is burdened. Burdened by the stress of deciding and the success or failure of the outcome. Certainly one of the joys of childhood is *not* having to decide, *not* having to make certain kinds of choices. And even if the parent is only giving lip service to the idea of choice, the illusion of choice still burdens the child.

Meals in American are often a smorgasbord of choice. Gone are the days when it was meat loaf or nothing. Now it can be three kinds of carry-out food or stops at two different fast food restaurants. My own children, upon returning from a Club Med–type vacation, wondered, "Why can't we have a buffet for supper?" I was amused a few years ago to see an ad promoting a two-tiered oven. Before: The family is at war about what to have for dinner. After: The family eats in peace with the adults' meal in the top oven and pizza for the smiling kids in the bottom.

Not only does open-ended and inappropriate choosing create anxiety, it also, and most significantly, begins to blur the lines that should define a child's place in the world. Little by little, the line between what's real and what's pretend gets blurred. Is little Sammy really choosing between a PT Cruiser and a Jeep Cherokee? Does he really believe he's making this choice? Life is a challenge for the child in this environment. He has no touchstone of what's real and what isn't. There are too many shades of gray.

High-maintenance children feel they exist at the center of things, that they deserve attention and focus. This perspective begins when a child is small. An entitled child rarely endures power struggles; he is simply indulged. Demands are met. Parents begin to focus on their child's feelings—how disappointed she'll feel if we go without her, how sad he'll feel if he doesn't do well—rather than seeing various events as important learning experiences. Parents' impulses to consider their child's feelings are well meaning. These parents are, after all, devoted to their children and sensitive to their children's needs. Unfortunately, over time, their focus begins to backfire, as their children miss out on the kind of experiences that stimulate emotional growth and resilience.

On the one hand, entitled children are often given grand responsibilities that are inappropriate and hollow (for example, "Where should we go on vacation?") while they are robbed of any actual responsibilities that entail real control of their lives, control that would entail consequences (for example, "It's too bad you left your homework until the last minute. You'll just have to tell the teacher you didn't finish it").

As an experienced high school guidance counselor recently told me, "This is the most overmanaged, overnagged, overindulged generation I've ever seen." It's that kind of parenting that encourages entitlement.

I recently had a parent tell me about her five-year-old who was creating disruptions in her kindergarten class. The teacher had called her in for a conference and described the daughter's refusal to cooperate, to wait her turn, and keep silent when required. And the child occasionally used foul language. The mother was terribly embarrassed. But when she described the situation to me and I enquired about the daughter's behavior at home, the mother said that her daughter regularly used bad language. "I don't know what she's thinking. I never would have spoken like that to my mother." She had never thought about *why* she never would have spoken that way to her mother, and what the consequences would have been if she did. When she appreciated the fact that she didn't use that kind of language as a child because "her mother would never have put up with it," she recognized that her child had come to realize that she would put up with it. And that was the information she needed to begin to change the situation.

Why is this happening? Where are all these high-maintenance children coming from? Why are parents, who are at heart really sensible and thoughtful people, allowing their children behaviors they know their own parents would never have tolerated? Why do so many parents find themselves in situations where they feel their own children are more in charge than they themselves?

For many parents it all begins with a beautiful baby romper that's only $16.95. Now that's not much to spend to make your already adorable baby look even more adorable. What a great feeling! For only about seventeen dollars you can delight yourself and your baby. It's pleasurable, it's satisfying, and it's fun. At first it's cheap. In a few years, it's a little Tonka toy while you're at the stationery store. And a candy bar while you're grocery shopping. Some Pokémon comics at the deli (after all, she is *reading*). And some fun jewelry from the Gap. And so on. Gradually you get sucked into a certain acceptance of your role as someone with an important job—to make your child happy. Who could have guessed how deep this river could be! And endless! And in thirty years, when they're unhappy, you may even find yourself paying for their psychotherapy!

In the end, of course, it's too much. Too much stuff. We all know in our hearts that a toddler is better off with a bowl and a spoon on the kitchen floor than in a room that's stuffed with a million toys. Your five-year-old will have more fun with the box than the computer that came in it. A teenager doing a research project is better off with a few good primary sources or reliable bookmarked Web sites. Unstructured use of the Internet is overwhelming; it's just too much information, too many choices with no quality controls.

It is harder for us, as parents, to draw the line. We're fighting a much bigger battle than our own parents. We weren't marketed to as our own children are. Every television show that appeals to children is spiked with commercials. We all know the rhythm of it: The advertisers begin in earnest in the fall, just after Halloween, hoping to lay claim to the must-have toy of the holiday season. Children, of course, are totally undiscriminating when it comes to acquiring toys. My own daughter came up to me one evening, asking for a particular toy she'd just seen advertised on TV. I asked her why she wanted it. She looked me as if I had sprouted wings.

Not only are children victimized by overt ads, there are now also "product placements" that speak to them subtly in films and television shows. Product placements are when advertisers arrange to have their products placed in an advantageous and visible setting in the media. These placements are becoming more popular because you can't skip the commercial with a click of the remote. So that, say, your little boy sees that his favorite film character drinks a certain kind of cola, or the characters on a children's sitcom use a certain brand of shampoo. It's difficult for children, particularly small children, to make distinctions between what's real life and what's television. Product placement makes it even more of a challenge.

Alas, even Elmo has taken the bait. On a *Sesame Street* show aired in April 2001, the *New York Times* reported that Elmo says, "Computers are great! You can use them to get e-mail from your friends!" Elmo may not know that his show is underwritten by AOL.

Magazines do their part to stimulate consumer lust among the young. The *New York Times* recently did a survey of teen magazines, their target audiences, and distinctive messages. The "message" of Condé Nast's *Teen Vogue* is "Fourteen-year-old girls can—and deserve to!—wear three-thousand-dollar couture dresses just like the grown-up supermodels." The culture of magazines in particular seems to revel in materialism and consumerism.

Vogue is for Mom, but *Elle Girl, YM,* and *Teen* magazine (Message as quoted from publicity material: "Transforming from a makeup-and-boys bible to a shopping-and-celebrity bible for the maturing girl and her maturing budget") all point the young woman toward consumerism as a kind of secular religion. Teenage magazines offer advertisers the best way to attract adolescent consumers while they are young and keep them. As Kevin G. Umeh, the president of Element, a market research firm that studies the buying patterns of teenagers, says, "Teenagers are avaricious consumers. They don't have to pay rent, they don't have to pay for health insurance, so their income is almost entirely disposable. They generally don't save. The trend is spend, spend, spend. And advertisers love to get them young because the chances they can keep them for life are good." As James McNeal, professor of marketing at Texas

A&M University, who has been studying children's consumer behavior for thirty years, told *Newsweek,* preteens have become the "powerhouse" of the kids' market, spending close to $14 billion a year.

It's easy to see how, materially, children become suffocated and spoiled. They're simply given too many things. But there's another, perhaps more interesting contributing factor to the plague of indulgence.

There has been a gradual shift in our culture in which advocacy has morphed into entitlement. In certain socioeconomic groups, advocacy is a critical and essential force that works toward true democracy. Parents mobilize and a poor school district is given grant money; the power of a coalition of disabled people forces public theaters to allow admittance to people in wheelchairs. These actions help to make access to life's pleasure and opportunities more fairly distributed.

Unfortunately, in upper socioeconomic groups, advocacy has sometimes mutated into a sophisticated grab for the best and the most.

As parents become more knowledgeable about developmental issues, as well as more busy and frantic and distracted—trying to balance a life, a career, a family—they use the consumer skills they've acquired, and blur the line between what's right and fair, and what's possible. They begin to ask, "What am I getting out of this teacher, this tutor, this board of ed, this school?"

For example, children with ADHD and other disabilities are allowed extended times to take certain standardized tests such as the SAT. For a disabled child, these kinds of accommodations level the playing field. For a child who is not disabled, extended time could, obviously, be an advantage. Since the IDEA

(Individuals with Disabilities Education Act) was modified in 1991, the number of children diagnosed with these disorders has exponentially increased, particularly among the upper socioeconomic strata. In 1991, the Educational Testing Service received eighteen thousand requests for extended time for test takers; in 1997, the number had jumped to forty-two thousand. Certainly we can be grateful that better screening for learning difficulties identifies more children who need such accommodations. Nonetheless, it's telling that the two mainstream (non–learning disabled) schools with the highest number of learning disabled students in the country, *Talk* magazine reveals, are two extremely competitive, highly selective high schools: Dalton in New York and the Crossroads School in California.

There's another case of this kind of hyperadvocacy that's been in the news lately. Krissy Keefer, a modern dancer, choreographer, and teacher, has filed a discrimination suit with the San Francisco Human Rights Commission. She contends that her daughter, Frederika, was barred from the San Francisco Ballet's School of Ballet beginning classes because she has what her mother describes as a "short, athletic body." Frederika, age eight, tried out with sixty-one other children and was one of eighteen dancers not accepted for classes.

The San Francisco Ballet publishes in its brochure criteria for the selection of incoming students. These include "a well-proportioned body, a straight and supple spine, legs turned out from the hip joint, and correctly arched feet. All beginners are accepted on a trial basis."

This seems quite straightforward—like a bias in favor of tall basketball players—but because the city of San Francisco denies money to organizations that discriminate on the basis of body type, Ms. Keefer feels that she has a case against the company.

Referring to the city's antidiscrimination laws, she says, "That is the only legal grounds I have. Without that, I would just be a disgruntled mother."

That's an extreme case of a mother trying to change the world to suit her child. Few of us would go that far. But how far is appropriate? Is it really wrong to use the system to get your child an advantage? To hold a child back a year from beginning kindergarten to give him an advantage over his peers? To demand extra test time for a trumped-up "disability" so a B+ student can become an A one? To fight for that honor roll bumper sticker and, ultimately, that Ivy League decal in the back windshield? Parents must, of course, weigh these issues for themselves, but I can tell you for certain that vanity sizing and its ultimate result—entitlement—does damage your child.

First of all, it's a breach of trust and a loss of connection to praise unreasonably. Most children are aware of the truth. They usually know where they stack up against their peers both academically and athletically. Children have an uncanny knack for sniffing out the truth, and they respect and trust an adult who is honest. I've seen this in my work with children in the hospital. For example, I once treated a young boy with cystic fibrosis. Out of love and denial, his parents had avoided telling him about his disease. At eight years of age, he enjoyed fencing and his parents seized upon this interest—a sign of normality—and praised his fencing in an almost compulsive way. It was almost as if the parents used the fencing to deny the reality of their son's illness. The boy knew that something was very seriously wrong with him. He felt frightened and alone. The praise had more to do with what the parents needed than what the child achieved. The praise rang hollow, as the boy was well aware, and it only served to amplify his overall anxiety about his mysterious condition.

There is often an implied message in extravagant praise. A parent sometimes puts a child on a pedestal because they worry that maybe he's not all that good, all that smart, all that talented. Like the boy with cystic fibrosis, a child who's praised lavishly for average accomplishments becomes suspicious. At a certain age, children begin to appreciate what is appropriate praise and what is bogus. They realize that there's something unreal about Dad cheering wildly when all they've done is pass the basketball, or Mom gushing about a truly mediocre painting. This kind of extravagant praise creates a sense that everyone is living a lie, and that the entire family must collude in order to preserve some mysterious balance.

There's yet another problem with vanity sizing. Some children come to believe it. They like the praise. Who doesn't, up to a point? They enjoy the attention and accolades. With these children praise that was intended to foster a sense of self-esteem derails and ends up fostering self-centeredness and self-absorption. This is the child who, on a visit to the pediatrician behaves as though possessed, biting the doctor, spitting at the nurse, and thrashing uncontrollably. Nonetheless, at the end of the visit, she's given a "happy face" sticker and a trip to Toys R Us. These children come to believe that they're wonderfully accomplished, even in areas where they're not doing that well at all. Their egos become inflated.

Ironically, this sort of child can sometimes seem more successful than he is because there are many instances where his confidence can mask poor performance. He's the first to raise his hand, even though his answers are often poorly thought out or just plain wrong. He has little respect for hard work, because he's learned that only *results* count, not process.

Appreciating the subtleties of social boundaries is a critical skill in life—a skill that many high-maintenance children never master. These children often lose the significance of social boundaries in relationships, especially with adults.

I heard recently from a teacher who was astounded by the behavior of one of her ninth-graders. She hadn't had time to correct an exam, which had been given the day before. This student approached her after class and suggested, "I have a 'free' this period. Why don't we go to the library together and go over my exam now?" Behaving like a CEO of a Fortune 500 company rather than a child, the boy was oblivious to the fact that his suggestion overstepped his role as a student.

I saw another instance of this inability to appreciate appropriate social nuances on a recent ski vacation with my family. A famous television news anchor was staying at the same resort, along with his wife, children, and two grandsons. A girl of about eleven approached him and introduced herself as the editor of her middle-school newsletter. She lingered too long and was observed chatting up the gentleman on several subsequent occasions. Clearly bemused, the anchorman was graceful and, following the instincts of a media-savvy performer, used the girl's brashness to his own advantage, asking, "Now, where's my little journalist?" and, "What happened to my rambunctious reporter?"

Other hotel guests were discomfited by the child's behavior. We've all seen people like this girl who, as adults, have difficulty in their relationships with others because they simply can't read signals of what's appropriate and what isn't. This child was oblivious to her effect on others, and filled with an unshakable conviction that she inhabited the red-hot center of the universe.

Most adults would find this sort of behavior offensive, but this child had clearly learned, presumably from home, that her interests, her goals, her desires come first.

While vanity sizing occurs routinely in the classroom or on the playing field, entitlement begins at home. Children sense that a huge trophy or 110 percent on a spelling test may be undeserved but it doesn't trouble them in any lasting way. But vanity sizing and extravagant praise at home has the potential to distort a child's sense of himself and his place in the world. A parent is the child's touchstone to what is true and real in life. Children who grow up uncertain of where a line should be drawn and unsure of what is exceptional as opposed to what is simply good, live with a fragile sense of self.

Entitlement is seen at its most noxious within the confines of family life because, while it corrodes a child's sense of self, it also corrodes the peace and pleasure of the unconditional freedom of the home. Home should be a place where everyone—parents, children, and pets—can let their hair down and put their feet up. Of course, there's the yelling and the cat puke and the sibling skirmishes. But that's the point. The last thing there should be at home is performance. A performance-powered house is the cradle of entitlement. When the parents feel the relentless obligation always to perform—to be on call to praise, to react, to listen, to guide, to encourage—the child begins to feel that his existence is the subject of endless interest, amusement, and delight. In fact, life at home becomes "The Little Johnny Show"!

I often joke that parents should be "space-occupying lesions" in their own home. "Space-occupying lesion" is a term used in medicine to describe a mass when we don't really know what it is. We know there's something there: We can palpate it or see it on x-ray or CAT scan or an MRI. It could be a vascular anomaly, a cyst, a tumor . . . We just don't know. Parents sometimes need to be space-occupying lesions. They need to talk on the phone (or try to), take a nap, read, clean a closet—be a background to their children's lives whenever they can. They need to seize the opportunity to do nothing when it presents itself. Sometimes organizing a playdate, a trip to the movies, or a discussion of a good subject for an English essay can just be put off while the child finds something to do on his own. It is important that a child learn to find something to do on his own. It may even be a relief for him.

Parents are not exclusively and entirely to blame for the entitlement of their children. Our culture encourages a kind of "disconnect" that almost forces children to build barriers between themselves and the world—to lose empathy for others and pave the way to entitlement. For one thing, our frantic lifestyle, pressured, anonymous, and goal-oriented, encourages kids to distance themselves from others. They're busy, they're on the run, and they may have no connection with neighbors and little connection with relatives. They're used to dealing with bureaucracy, and they are forced to adjust to being anonymous in a host of situations. They may have "second lives" on the Internet, where they've learned that they can be anyone they want and the "screen names" they chat with are anyone they claim to be.

The economy too forces children to wall themselves off from certain feelings. The enormous contrast between rich and poor in the United States is difficult for a child to understand. With the lion's share of wealth concentrated in the hands of a few, countless others, at home and abroad, live in desperate poverty. Why should one family be homeless when my friend or I have two or three homes? Children typically react to this kind of disparity in two ways: They feel guilty and/or ashamed.

Either of these feelings is painful, particularly if you feel responsible for the cause. Ultimately children are forced to distance themselves from these feelings as a simple gesture of self-preservation.

Children are also exposed to the tremendous suffering of third world countries on TV. They see starving children and families driven from their homes by war and natural disasters. The constant repetition of images that are distressing and offer no hope of a solution trivializes the real suffering seen and eventually saturates children's psyches. Impotent and confused, they distance themselves from what they see.

It's not only the real-life terrors that build scar tissue on vulnerable children. It's also the "entertainment" that relies on violence. Repeated images of violence, domestic violence, fantasy violence, "docudramas" that rely on shocking incidents and, perhaps worst of all, the "reality" TV, including shows such as *Cops* and *Rescue 911*, fill children's heads with terribly distressing images and give them no outlet for the confusion and fear these scenes create. Furthermore, this violence, whether on television, in a movie, or in a computer game, has become so routine that many adults don't even flinch. But this kind of violence is terribly arousing: It speaks to our "frog brain," our fight-or-flight impulse. Unable to have any resolution to the emotions triggered by what we see, we become desensitized. We also become more poised to accept aggression as a viable means of conflict resolution. In subtle ways, it causes us to overreact to frustration in our own lives. This is one of the reasons that there are so many instances of road rage or air rage. People are stimulated by a steady diet of violence: They are prepared to pounce, and when presented with an opportunity, they find it hard to resist.

Most of us spend little time watching Jerry Springer as he

band-leads mothers of scantily clad, tattooed teenager daughters who shout epithets such as "slut" and "whore" at one another. But many of our children, left to their own devices, find these shows mesmerizing. Perhaps you've watched one of those real-life cop shows or even a film of a surgery on television. The people involved, the patient or the victim, are terrible to watch. We can't take our eyes off it, and yet we're horrified. We've lost empathy. We've entered the depersonalized realm of voyeurism. We watch that guy getting his eyeball sliced, or the woman trying to shield herself from her husband's blows as her children watch, crying. Though we watch, we simply can't bear to put ourselves in that spot: It's just too painful. And we're adults! Children are deeply affected by such sights and the knowledge that adults seem to show little or no reaction to them.

Factors that might mitigate against this walling off or desensitization—loving supervision, lots of family contact, consistent rules and obligations, rituals—simply don't exist for many children. Thus the desensitized child—the child who has not had the opportunity to explore how he or she feels, who cannot recognize the emotional torque of an experience—becomes disconnected from internal states, his own and others. This disconnect discourages empathy: It's much more comfortable to focus on the non-feeling aspect of an experience, on the what, the who, the where and the how than on the subtle, emotional complexity of an event. This disconnect is fertile ground for entitlement.

Many of us have to work to avoid fostering entitlement in our children. The unprecedented prosperity we enjoy and the overwhelming demands on our time often make it difficult to say, "that's too expensive," "too far," "too late," "too inconvenient." Most of us feel guilty that we don't spend more time with our children, and we use money and the granting of privileges to assuage our guilt.

As we all know, there is a downside to luxury and indulgence, and it's far more damaging to children than to adults, who at least may have some concept of what it takes to make money and what it costs to live. Constant indulgence paradoxically leads to a loss of pleasure. As Nietzsche observed, "Possessions are generally diminished by possession." Genuine gratification and satisfaction depend on at least some measure of delay, denial, and anticipation. As Alain de Botton put it so beautifully in *How Proust Can Change Your Life: Not a Novel,*

> If the rich are fortunate in being able to travel to Dresden as soon as the desire to do so arises, or to buy a dress just after they have seen it in a catalog, they are cursed because of the speed with which their wealth fulfills their desires. No sooner have they thought of Dresden than they can be on a train there; no sooner have they seen a dress than it can be in their wardrobe. They therefore have no opportunity to suffer the interval between desire and gratification which the less privileged endure, and which, for all its apparent unpleasantness, had the incalculable benefit of allowing people to know and fall deeply in love with paintings in Dresden, hats, dressing gowns, and someone who isn't free this evening.

The Wall Street Journal had an enlightening article recently tracing the changes in holiday gift-giving habits from the 1900s to today. One hundred years ago, even a wealthy woman would yearn for little more than a tortoise shell comb as a holiday gift. A child would be delighted by an orange or some candy. Of course you can see where this is going. If you're reading this book, you probably have children, and you probably faced a "wish list" last holiday season, perhaps one posted on the Internet for the convenience of friends and relatives, that might have featured a Nintendo or Sony PlayStation, a computer, a kickboard scooter, a Tamagotchi and Digimon, a mountain bike, Barney merchandise, and, of course, Barbie and her houses, cars, and endless wardrobe.

Entitlement really can't be cured; high maintenance can only be avoided. It calls for a bit less adoration and immediate gratification. And perhaps a few chores and a summer job. Fewer and fewer young people are working during the summer. As parents and students feverishly build résumés that will stand out, they forgo jobs like lifeguarding, cashiering, and waitressing for personally enriching experiences like working with natives in Costa Rica, trekking the Nepali mountains, or perhaps taking an advance course at a prestigious school. Among young men ages sixteen to nineteen, the summer employment rate in 1999 was the lowest since the Bureau of Labor Statistics started keeping track in 1948. In a *New York Times* article, a Georgetown University junior is quoted as saying his time is worth more than the ten dollars an hour he could expect to be paid at a typical summer job. He was spending the summer at a South Korean university. But he may wish he'd taken the job. More and more professionals and graduate schools are taking a skeptical view of these too perfect résumés. I know of several department chiefs at teaching hospitals who have chosen the hamburger-cook-turned-B+ medical student over the A+ achiever who helped map the human genome. In their words, "These guys smell of high maintenance."

As David Davenport, the ex-president of Pepperdine University in California, remarks "To spend more time reading American history and playing soccer is not the same as getting out in the world and having experiences." He admits to the *New York Times* that he irritates faculty by insisting "he learned more frying doughnuts in his father's bakery than in any university." As he claims, "We're crowding out the well-rounded development of our children."

Moral Bankruptcy

Maryanne is a polished and professional textile designer. Her husband is an attorney, and she has a successful business working with decorators to create beautiful fabrics used in draperies and linens. Maryanne lives in Manhattan, and her three-year old daughter, Beth, is the apple of her eye. Last year, Beth was in the process of applying to a prestigious nursery school in their Manhattan neighborhood. Competition was rigorous, and Maryanne saw Beth's acceptance as the first hurdle she would leap in getting her child's life off to a good start. So she got a copy of the Stanford-Binet test—an intelligence test whose results are valid only when it's administered to an unprepared child—and spent a few evenings with her daughter, talking about the simple problems and questions on the test and explaining how a round shape fits in a round hole, etc. Maryanne felt sheepish about this but justified it by saying, "Well, they have to admit a certain number of kids and how the heck do you distinguish between three-year-olds? Beth is bright and well behaved, and would certainly do well at the school. So why not?"

Michael is a freshman in high school. A good student and a friendly boy, Michael is also a very good lacrosse player. It's a varsity team tryout week, and Michael has been at school late every day. Now it's Thursday. He has a paper due Friday on The Grapes of Wrath. *He's read most of the book, but he has done nothing about the paper. A poor grade could affect his average, which is teetering at a high B and could conceivably keep him out of the Advanced Placement English class next year. His mother is frantic. She's been bugging Michael to get going on the paper, but she also recognizes that he just doesn't have much time. While Michael is at tryouts, she researches five good Internet sites relating to the book and finds some excellent material. She does an outline of a paper and, because now she's really into it, she comes up with a good beginning sentence and drafts a couple of paragraphs. Is it the right thing to do? She shrugs. "He actually could write a better paper than me. But how can he possibly get through tryout week plus do all this work? It's really asking too much of him. And besides, it's just an outline and some references. I don't know many mothers who wouldn't do the same."*

Pam and her daughter Laurie, who is nine, are shopping. They're at the counter in the designer department at Neiman Marcus when Mom pulls a dress out of the bag and says she wants to return it. It's an expensive black dress that flatters

Pam. Laurie looks at her mom in surprise. She knows her mom wore the dress over the weekend to a cocktail party. But Laurie soon sees that the tags are still on the dress, and the woman behind the counter will never know that it's been worn. "I decided it's a bit too much for the budget," Pam explains. The saleswoman smiles and issues a refund on Pam's credit card. Pam winks at Laurie and Laurie smiles back.

Jackie is rushing through the grocery store with her seven-year-old and her toddler. She needs to get things for dinner and also items for the cupcakes she's supposed to bake for tonight's school fair. She will barely have time to squeeze the baking in, but she's promised to do it. The toddler spots his favorite cookies and begins to wail, thrashing and throwing things out of the cart. Jackie does not want to buy the cookies. Her kids eat too many sweets already, and, if the cookies are in the house, she knows she'll eat them herself. She grabs the bag of cookies, rips it open, gives her toddler two, jams the bag back onto the shelf, and rushes down the aisle. Her seven-year-old watches in silence.

Does this sort of thing matter? Is anyone the worse for it? Haven't we all done something similar to these parents—cut corners, told white lies, cheated a little on our taxes, fudged a bit? Isn't it a drag to examine these minor moral transgressions? Besides, everybody does this kind of stuff. And, of course, you have to expect some misbehavior from kids. They all eventually steal a candy bar from the deli, or write a bad word on the bathroom wall at school, right?

Sadly, too many children are learning that morality and common virtues such as honesty, respect for others, and courage don't really matter much any more.

A few months ago, a shocking incident at a Baltimore, Maryland, private school had area parents reeling. A lacrosse player at the school had sex with a fifteen-year-old girl, videotaped the act, and then played it for members of his team. He actually played it twice: once for a small group and then for a larger gathering of players. In the end, the boy was expelled, and thirty of the participants were suspended. Parents were shocked to find that young people would behave in that fashion. "Who would have thought," wondered one quoted mother, "that I'd have to one day sit my teenager down and tell him that it's not OK to have sex with a minor, tape it, and then show it to your friends?" Who, indeed? But, as an article in the *Washington Post* by Deborah M. Roffman, the author of *Sex and Sensibility* and a specialist in family life education who works with children, pointed out, it's the shock that's shocking. "The fact that these examples of precocious, unhealthy sexualization are not on most adults' radar screens—not even in their worst nightmares—speaks legions. For someone like me, who has been teaching about sexuality for more than thirty years, the surprise is in the surprise."

Of course, it's silly to suggest that a child who watches a parent return a worn dress will then perform in a sex videotape. But it is fair to claim that many parents today have disassociated themselves from taking responsibility for the moral upbringing of their children. The dissonance between what parents say and what they do can create a disquieting cynicism in their children. If Mr. Rogers, their teacher, and their parents insist that honesty is the best policy, but they see numerous instances of adults in their lives lying to gain some advantage, children are not stupid enough to believe that honesty really is the best policy. Idealism turned sour is cynicism. While insisting on academic rigor, many parents have abandoned moral rigor. Or they have made some effort at forming their children's character, but they haven't really taken into account the powerful undertow that's working against them.

Remember Gordon Gecko? He was the slick, rapacious wheeler and dealer in the movie *Wall Street*. Michael Douglas won an Oscar for playing the role of the man everybody loved to hate: the embodiment of the Reagan-era credo that "greed is good." Gecko, named for his reptilian ability to attack corporate targets and swallow them whole, was a stock speculator who succeeded by using illegal inside information to buy and sell other people's dreams, and make a lot of money along the way. He was a compelling and seductive role model for the young, ambitious Wall Street broker played by Charlie Sheen, who falls into Gecko's sphere of influence and instantly succumbs to the allure of risky deals and generous payoffs. While the film is a bit dated and heavy-handed, it's still thrilling to watch Michael Douglas swagger with the sheer power of greed and the single-mindedness of a man who's sacrificed humanity for money.

Of course the movie is a cautionary tale. In the end, Gecko doesn't triumph, and his protégé learns that money is the root of all evil—a lesson young Charlie Sheen's father had been trying to teach him ever since the opening scene.

Gordon Gecko made evil look good. But of course he was punished. Today there are plenty of people who make bad look good. Few are punished; to the contrary, they're often rewarded. Eminem has won four Grammys. His songs explore such themes as killing his wife and raping his mother. And there are weekly sensational headlines publicizing the extramarital affairs and illegal activities of celebrities. Unlike Gordon Gecko, who was ultimately humiliated and sent to prison, our erring celebrities are usually rewarded with a fat book contract and an endless stream of invitations. Our children watch them succeed at misbehavior. Celebrities they might have been eager to condemn when they were five can look pretty smart when they're fourteen. This is the tide that parents have to fight. Obviously, it takes more sophistication, effort, and will than our parents needed in an era when the "itsy-bitsy teeny-weeny yellow polka-dot bikini" was a shock and sitcom parents were only allowed to sleep in twin beds.

Most parents get off to a good start with their children, emphasizing proper behavior and pointing to lessons in everything from "The Three Little Pigs" to *Mr. Rogers' Neighborhood.* One of the preoccupying tasks of parents of young children is to teach them a kind of social or "playground" morality: Don't hit your friend. You must share. You shouldn't hurt anyone's feelings. You can't take someone else's toy. You can't tell the lady she has a mustache, even if she does.

None of these admonitions really have to do with building character; they substitute a sort of "expedient" morality for a true moral compass. This kind of morality is, like other issues we've discussed, including learning and athletics, concerned far more with the *outcome* than the process. The girl won't be your friend if you hit her. If you share with him, he'll share with you. Will Beth get into preschool? Will Pam get the pleasure of wearing a dress for free? Will Michael retain his grade-point average? Will the community service count on your college application, and, if it doesn't, is it worth doing? How does this relatively benign behavior relate to children making and sharing a sex video? Of course, teenagers do stupid things and always have. But the callousness and disconnect of the behavior of the Baltimore students is pretty spectacular. And such behavior among young people is not that uncommon today.

Unfortunately, once children reach the upper elementary grades, or certainly middle school, a time when they really begin to form solid ideas of what kind of person they want to be and what really matters to them, direct or thoughtful ethical "education" has in too many cases been abandoned. Schools do take on the task of endless drug, alcohol, and possibly sex education, but for the most part, as far as the older child is concerned, it's devoid of moral and ethical content. I am not stepping here into the argument about whether or not moral training belongs in school curricula. I am simply saying that it currently is not a part of most students' formal education, and that leaves only one place for children to learn how to behave ethically: the home. While most Americans agree that this is the system they prefer, too many then ignore their obligations as parents to step into the breach or, perhaps more commonly, ignore the fact that the way they live their lives is teaching a moral lesson to their children. After all, moral training goes on whether it is a subject or not. We are teaching our children by the examples we set, the things we say and, more important, the things we do.

No doubt the amorality we see among young people begins with the disconnect that I have described in the previous chapters. The distressing gap between haves and have nots, the suffering of people in natural disasters or Third World countries, powerful and extreme violence on television that our children are exposed to on a daily basis, combined with a lack of mitigating factors, such as strong community connections, close and frequent contact with parents, a feeling that they're in control of their lives—these factors all foster an emotional disconnect. Children simply can't tolerate these endlessly disturbing stimuli, and so they shut down. A child who's learned to distance himself from emotionally charged situations will find it easier to videotape himself having sex than a child who feels embarrassment, shame, and dismay at the thought of making such a tape. Moreover, this child will find it easier to watch such a tape without protest. It's as though the children who watched the tape and those who behave in similar disassociated ways are completely out of touch with what preserves our dignity as humans, with empathy and morals.

There certainly seems to be a decline in empathy for others among many young people. Empathy is identification with, or the vicarious experience of, the inner state of another. By allowing us to imagine and share what another person is feeling, empathy enables us to climb out of our own skin and into another's. Empathy is an important component of morality because it creates a social context: We are all in this together, and what you do to him you do to me. But as regularly confirmed by newspaper headlines, many young people sorely lack empathy, as demonstrated, in the extreme, by some youth crimes. In Brooklyn, for instance, three teenage boys described by neighbors as "nice kids" were arrested for dousing sleeping homeless men with gasoline and setting fire to them. As they were booked at the police station, according to the *New York Times* (newspaper photographs show them smiling), one of them explained, "We just like to harass the bums." These teens may be capable of selective empathy toward the family and neighbors who describe them as "nice kids," but they display a stunning lack of empathy for the suffering of the homeless men they set on fire. Of course, boys like these are casualties, too.

Even toddlers are capable of empathetic responses. But it's

too difficult for children to empathize if doing so means being paralyzed by negative emotions because they are unable do anything to change the troubling situation they encounter. For example, it's too painful to identify with a homeless man talking to himself. They begin to resent him, in fact, for making them feel distressed. That resentment, combined with parental neglect, lack of a moral compass, and the overstimulation of media violence too often finds its expression in horrid, meaningless cruelty.

Disconnect and lack of empathy, of course, don't *cause* immoral behavior. They simply create a precipitating condition. When trying to assess the mind-set of the boy involved in the case of the sex tape described above, a major consideration is the amount of sexual material young people are exposed to today. For example, you've probably never heard of the MTV television show *Undressed*. Few parents I've asked are familiar with the show. But if you have teenagers, they are probably well aware of it and may have seen it. It airs at variable times very early in the morning (1:30 or 2 A.M.) and features young people dressed in lingerie and leather having sex while their parents are out. Do they really have sex? Well, not quite. But it's a fine line. Here's the ad copy from the *Undressed* Web site: "You know you want it. A little late-night tease makes bedtime that much better. Add some playful intrigue to the mix and you've got yourself a dream come true. It all starts with a glance, a sexy stare—and from there? Get 'Undressed' and find out."

If you do a search for *Undressed* on the Internet, which many teens do because the air times for the show are irregular, you'll find links to sites featuring such subjects as "a thousand ways to masturbate" and tips on anal intercourse. In a bizarre juxtaposition, one link lists the site creator's favorite books, including

Harry Potter and the Goblet of Fire and (I apologize in advance for this, but I think most parents have no idea what's so readily available to their children) *A Hand in the Bush: The Fine Art of Vaginal Fisting*.

Sexual images flood the media, many directed to young people. And the provocative way that middle-and high school girls dress intensifies the sexual tension. The principal of a public high school in an affluent community told me he was extremely frustrated when it came to his school's dress code. He could insist that the girls not wear spaghetti straps, very short skirts, or shorts to school, but he certainly couldn't have a teacher measure skirt lengths. And, as he said, "I just wish their mothers would tell them it's inappropriate to wear a see-through shirt to school."

It's not sex that's the problem. That's been around for a long time. It's the context. Today, teens and children are playing out their natural impulses in an atmosphere that glorifies celebrity, exhibitionism, and total personal exposure. They exploit and are exploited by one another and the culture. Perhaps it's fine that Jennifer Lopez wants to show off her breasts, but must it be on national TV? Of course, if she did it to insure a full and unwavering headshot as the *New Yorker* implied, I suppose we should applaud her cleverness. But while nudity and exhibitionism may translate into big bucks in Hollywood, it leads to trouble closer to home.

As Deborah Roffman, quoted earlier in connection with the high school sex video says, "The surprise is the surprise." You simply can't expose young people to countless hours of sexual content in television, films, and music without having some effect on their sexual behavior. Particularly because parents don't seem to have any mitigating role in interpreting these images and behaviors to their children. If your child watches

Undressed, you probably don't know. You are tired at night. You may go to bed before your child. Your child may be at a sleep-over, watching with friends. Few young people today are watching television with their parents. They're watching in their own rooms or alone in a "family" room while their parents are out, or working, or working out.

So it's fair to be horrified, but you shouldn't be shocked.

Inappropriate sexual behavior is only one bit of evidence that many children are lacking moral guidance. Another common, even epidemic issue is cheating. Recent research has shown that cheating in high schools and colleges has become a way of life for increasing numbers of students. In a survey cited by the *New York Times,* of twenty-one thousand students surveyed by the Josephson Institute of Ethics, 70 percent of high school students and 54 percent of middle-school students admitted that they had cheated on an exam. A comparable study in 1969—roughly thirty years earlier—found that about a third of high school students had cheated on a test. Moreover, about 60 percent of high school students let someone else copy their work in 1969 and nearly 100 percent did so thirty years later. A young man told me of a high school student he knows—a bright boy—who writes papers for other students for a fee. It's his version of a part-time job. As he explains it, the boy feels it's a good way to earn money because he's learning as he goes, his customers don't go to his school so he's not competing with himself for grades, and he's proud of the fact that both his real and his "shadow" grade-point averages are quite high.

Writing a paper for profit seems almost as old fashioned as a medieval guild these days. The Internet provides far more so-phisticated, convenient, and thrilling methods of cheating. You can type a term paper subject into any search engine and find thousands of sites like Cheaters.com or Papers-R-Us, offering papers for a fee. You can exchange science projects and solutions to math problems in chat rooms and share test questions and answers via e-mail. The more sophisticated and adventuresome cheaters can hack into school mainframes to alter transcripts. Perhaps you've heard of using cell phones to dial multiple-choice answers into alphanumeric pagers or storing all kinds of cheat-sheet information on highly evolved calculators. You can even, if you're absolutely determined to avoid studying, and if you're willing to research the latest technological possibilities, rely on devices that use infrared technology to send an answer from the back of the class to the front.

When did cheating become epidemic? Perhaps when it became relatively anonymous (i.e., materials on the Internet), or perhaps when it became relatively profitable. It hasn't helped that many parents feel that the goal of high school is winning a slot in an Ivy League college. Simplistic? Perhaps. But when parents and teachers themselves are cheating to "make things look better," why would they expect their children not to? In one *U.S. News* poll, twenty percent of adults thought doing homework for a child was fair. While many parents would be shocked indeed if their child made a sex video, fewer would be shocked if they were caught cheating.

Even the teachers are cheating. Cheating has become the winked-at technique that some educators are using to combat the crushing pressure they're under to deliver high test scores. As the *New York Times* trumpeted in a front-page headline: "Investigator Says Teachers in City Aided in Cheating." The article goes on to cite thirty-two New York City public schools that allegedly supplied answers to raise the scores of children taking standardized tests. Dozens of teachers and two principals were involved. There have also been recent reports, one in *The Wall*

Street Journal, of prestigious high schools, including prep schools, burnishing the applications of their students to increase their chances of being admitted to Ivy League colleges. You can't charge high tuitions if you don't get results.

It's difficult for children to learn moral lessons when they aren't taught any. Many parents have been blurring that line since their children were small. Do they pay the full airline fare or the "child's fare" when their children are just a half year too old? Have you paid the child's rate for a weeklong ski pass for your smallish fifteen-year-old? Have you helped him type a paper the night before, or have you let him deal with the consequences of not getting his work finished? Have you watched him beef up an application for a job or college with exaggerated or even made-up information? Have you complained about a teacher without even considering whether your child's behavior might be causing the problem? Few among us haven't run red lights, sworn at other drivers, or parked "just for a minute" in a handicapped space. *The New Yorker* had an amusing cartoon that points at this issue: A mother stands before a teacher's desk, holding a small child's hand. She says, "So what if he paid a classmate to do his homework—it was his own allowance."

Certainly my aim here is not to instill guilt or teach morality. If you do not think that a moral code is an important component to a happy, fulfilled life, I'm not going to convince you otherwise. Most educators, as well as philosophers, agree that children, like adults, need a sense that their life means something more than getting up, going to school, trying to get good grades, watching TV, and going to bed each day. Aristotle defined good character as the life of right conduct—right conduct in relation to other persons and in relation to one's self. He also held that character was a means to an end, a way of achieving the ultimate purpose of life. For him, that purpose was happiness.

If you believe that children need a solid base of core virtues, then it's important to remember that it's your job to teach them that code, not only when they're small but also as they grow. Moral values (such as respect for life and liberty, responsibility toward others, honesty, fairness, tolerance, courtesy, self-discipline, integrity, kindness, compassion, and courage) define the many ways of being a good person. Taken together, they are the moral heritage that one generation passes on to the next. Ethical literacy requires knowing these values.

Many of us are overwhelmed by the notion of teaching ethics. There are just too many choices, too many permutations of every situation. We're loath to make judgments. Perhaps we don't always know what is right, and what is right for one may not be right for all. But we can get the dialogue going early and maintain it. Ethical issues permeate every choice we make from whether to get a puppy to who sews our clothes or picks our coffee, or why you don't want to support the school bond. All are good points of departure for lessons about right and wrong, or better or worse.

If parents don't assume responsibility to teach them, these values will, like reading and writing during the Middle Ages, become lost. Certainly some youthful subgroups in this country are already in a medieval stage of moral development. For example, Cornell University historian Joan Jacobs Brumberg, author of *The Body Project,* a history of American girls, remarked to *Newsweek* that fifty years ago, when girls talked about self-improvement, they were thinking of doing good works or doing better in school. Now a girl's emphasis is more typically on her appearance. Looks, not behavior, have become a measure of self-worth.

In order to have a resilient moral code, children must understand what is morally right, and they must obey the impulse to behave correctly. The second factor, the impulse to behave correctly, is, of course, a conscience. Most people, whether they obey it or not, have a conscience—a little Jiminy Cricket voice that says, "Tell her she undercharged you" or "Don't repeat the gossip you just heard about the woman down the street."

I think it's important for parents to consider and appreciate that while children have a conscience, many children really don't know what is morally right. For example, in a study conducted by Who's Who Among American High School Students, 80 percent of high-achieving high schoolers admitted to having cheated at least once; half said they did not believe cheating was necessarily wrong. One college freshman told me, "You feel bad the first time you cheat, but then you get used to it."

In a 1988 survey conducted by the Rhode Island Rape Crisis Center, researchers asked one thousand seven hundred students in the sixth through ninth grades the following question: "Is it acceptable for a man to force a woman to have sex if he has spent money on her?" Twenty-four percent of the boys and 16 percent of the girls said yes. The researchers also asked, "Is it acceptable for a man to force a woman to have sex if they have been dating for more than six months?" Sixty-five percent of the boys and 47 percent of the girls said yes.

We can't expect children to behave correctly if they don't know what's right and what isn't. If our zeal to push our children toward success has compromised our responsibility also to educate them to be moral citizens, we may be winning a few battles but losing the war. As we've seen, some of the greatest satisfactions in life come from such intangibles as caring relationships, a sense of purpose, and adherence to a code of behavior that recognizes common goals and values. If our children are robbed of these satisfactions, no matter their "success," their lives may never be as full and pleasurable as we might wish.

The Big Backfires: Anxiety, Inhibition, and Adolescence

Parents, with the very best intentions, nudge and encourage and, yes, push their children because they believe that their children need it. As we discussed in previous chapters, a variety of motives drive us to help our children "be the best that they can be." Most parents think that the worst that can happen is that it won't work: The pushing won't yield results, our daughter won't make the honor roll, and our son won't be team captain. But there are other, more serious, drawbacks to pushing a child to achieve, or even just to be something that they're not.

There's no doubt that the pushed child can suffer from anxiety and inhibition. When pressure to perform builds, many people respond by shutting down. You have probably felt this yourself. You have to give a critical presentation or hold an important meeting. It's natural to be nervous. But sometimes we feel so nervous that it compromises our performance; sometimes we even feel that we simply can't proceed. We lose confidence and faith in our ability to perform.

Anxiety plays a large role in our ability to perform, and it's helpful for parents to understand anxiety and how it can affect our children. It's also important to understand how parents can unwittingly create anxiety in their children.

Though we're not really certain what causes anxiety, it's commonly accepted as a feeling that is wired into us as humans. It serves a natural and adaptive function and, in terms of evolution, it has probably helped to keep us safe from predators. In addition to this natural, adaptive anxiety, there is also learned anxiety. This is the kind of anxiety that's associated with a past experience. Anyone who has been in a pediatrician's office has no doubt witnessed learned anxiety. A baby is brought in for a checkup. As soon as he senses where he is, he begins to cry. He's associated through sensory cues—smells, sounds, sights—that this is a place he doesn't like. Perhaps he got an injection last time. Or perhaps he simply doesn't like to be undressed. He's learned to become anxious the minute his mother enters the office. A dog will sometimes evidence dramatic learned anxiety: When the suitcases come out of the closet, some dogs will begin to pace and salivate, or hide in anticipation of a trip.

Finally, there's anxiety that's learned through conditioning with a particular situation or event. The classic example of this is the Pavlovian example, where dogs were trained to salivate when they heard a bell in anticipation of food. Eventually, they salivated at the bell, food or not. Some theorists have determined that panic attacks and claustrophobia are coupled responses. A person might believe that, for example, a subway ride causes his panic attacks. In fact, it could be that the person suffered a panic attack in the subway, was unable to get out, and now associates any subway ride with a panic attack.

Children are born with a natural temperament that affects their general anxiety level. Some children startle easily, are alarmed by loud noises, and are frightened by novel environments. Others are more placid. They'll sleep through anything, smile at the mailman, and barely react to the various stimuli of a busy household. One thing is certain: Whatever the baby's innate temperament, his attachment to his caregiver is a mitigating factor in his anxiety level. If a stranger approaches, a baby sitting in his parent's lap is likely to be less frightened than the baby who's sitting alone in the car seat. If the baby falls and Mother smiles at her and kisses the hurt, the baby will probably be less upset than if she'd fallen while alone. A child who grows up in a secure, predictable household, where the experiences of pain, hunger, discomfort, and anger are attended to by a loving figure—that child will be better prepared to meet the vicissitudes of life. A secure attachment with a caregiver is also believed to have a biological impact upon the developing infant: It helps create a solid base from which to experiment and learn about the world.

When parents begin to push, they risk damaging the secure attachment that cushions children as they make their way through the world. Children whose parents are focused primarily on outcome—making the honor roll, making the team, making the college—learn, explicitly or implicitly, that if they don't hold up their end of the bargain, their parents will love them less. This scenario is grossly simplified, of course. But there is evidence that children who are pressured, or who have learned to focus only on goals, are less creative, spontaneous, and eager to experiment. They tend to be anxious and inhibited. One study by Brandeis University psychologist Teresa Amabile asked twenty-two girls to make "silly collages." Some of the girls competed for prizes and some didn't. Seven artists independently rated the girls' work. The children who were trying to win a prize produced work that was much less creative—less spontaneous, complex, and varied—than the children who were simply creating for the pleasure of what they could achieve.

To develop a strong sense of self, children must feel free to fail. This is a critical component of any achievement. No one, child or adult, can succeed without being willing to risk failure. As James Joyce said, "Mistakes are the portals of discovery." Children become anxious when they are pressured into achieving goals rather than concentrating on the process of an activity. They are more likely to give up, or find themselves unable to do their best, than their unpressured peers.

Jack was excited about his third-grade science project. He was interested in frogs, had one as a pet, and knew where he could get a tadpole. He wanted to watch the tadpole grow and chart its growth. His dad thought the project was too simple and boring. Why not make the project more interesting by putting tadpoles in different environments to see which one grew fastest? You could set up three or four tanks. One would be warm, one cool, one would have tap water, and one would have water from the stream behind their house with some small plants tossed in. Jack could do daily charts to keep track of the growth. While Jack was thrilled with his father's attention to his project—what child wouldn't be—he gradually lost his excitement about the endeavor. When he tentatively made suggestions, his father, however gently, rebuffed them. Jack felt, and rightly so, that the project wasn't really his. It was his father's. He stopped making any kind of suggestions, and simply followed his father's directions on how to fill out the chart each evening. By the time the project was finished and handed in, Jack had lost all interest in frogs and felt uncomfortable about the good grade he got. His father felt that the project had been a big success, and never guessed that his efforts had actually pushed Jack away from the very goal his father had for him: an eagerness to compete and succeed.

Parents must support their child through success and failure. However, they need to try, to some degree, to distance themselves from the results of their child's efforts and focus instead on the effort. Jack's father, for instance, would have done so much better to simply ask questions about Jack's science project. What was Jack planning? How did he intend to set his project up? Where would he get the tadpole? Had he managed to find some books on frogs that would be helpful? If he had participated in this way, Jack would have relished his father's interest but would have not become inhibited by his father's directives.

Sometimes parents' intense focus on young children's activities robs them of the opportunity to fail and learn. Children are rarely on their own these days. They're on supervised playdates, organized sporting teams, and group lessons and activities. We're encouraged to become almost overly involved in their lives and activities. I spoke recently with two fourteen-year-old boys who occasionally arranged informal paddleball games. They realized in the course of the conversation that they had never played a sport—a baseball game, a basketball game, anything—completely independently, without a coach or parent involved. They are typical of today's children.

Children feel that our eyes are always upon them. We're ready to praise or correct. We've come to believe that our involvement is critical to their success. The backfire is that when the child comes to believe this, too, he will have a very hard time succeeding.

Some pressured children seem to defy the scenarios described above. They perform beautifully. They put their best effort into pleasing their parents. They make the honor roll, strive to do their best, and in general seem to be just want the parents want. Until they become adolescents. Then, as many disappointed and perplexed parents can tell you, it's a whole new game.

The bad news is that, in general, normal adolescent development involves moving from a hardworking, compliant, industrious kid to a rebellious, unpredictable, sometimes insolent young adult. The good news is that there is a range of normal adolescent behaviors: At one end of the spectrum is the child who moves easily through the teen years. Yes, this does happen and you could get lucky. Many developmental specialists have noted that the other end of the spetrum—the stereotype of the angry, out-of-control, self-destructive teenager—is just that: a stereotype. In any event, wherever your child registers on the behavior Richter scale, the best news is that the teen years ultimately end and, angry or cheerful, the teen eventually becomes an adult. In the meantime, the experience of the teen years, yours and your child's, will depend in large part on the relationship that you've formed with your child, and on your own particular style in the "dance" of parenting. A solid, respectful relationship, while it can't be guaranteed to keep difficulties at bay, will at least be your "money in the bank" when you face the teen years.

If parents could only have a crystal ball and could look ahead, beyond the Legos and the Play-Doh, to the young man or woman they will be living with and loving in the teen years, I think they might be more introspective about some aspects of

The World of Almost Perfect

Josh and Max are eleven-year-old twins. Twice a week they are awakened at four-thirty in the morning, dressed in the dark, and driven to hockey practice. They eat Pop Tarts en route. Their father is very enthusiastic about the boys' hockey—he calls them his double threat—and he's gotten them expensive gear bags and new sticks for their birthday. The boys' mother is ambivalent. Josh and Max both have fallen asleep at their desks at school in the past weeks. But, shrugging, she claims, "They just love it. And their dad is so proud of them."

Ginny is a sophomore at a prestigious private school in New York. Her older brother attends an Ivy League college, their father's alma mater. Ginny is getting C's and B's in school, trol and nothing more out of control than adolescence. Early adolescence in particular is about loss of control. Most dramatically, bodies are changing, seemingly overnight. Friendships, the cement of childhood, are dissolving and re-forming. Teachers' expectations are changing. The ground is shifting beneath your feet.

A friend tells the story of sharing a pizza at a local roller rink with a group of fifth-graders. It somehow became known that she weighed sixty-nine pounds. One of the boys elbowed his buddy and said loudly, "Can you believe it? Ann weighs sixty-nine! Get it?" The group laughed uproariously. The friend laughed with them. She can remember to this day what she was wearing, who was at the table, what they were eating, and most of all she can remember the vast discomfort of having no idea what the joke was about. She only recently realized that she might not have been the only one who didn't get it.

That's what adolescence is like: desperately wishing that you'd "get it." And feeling out of control when so often you don't.

Parents of adolescents are dealing with control, too. There's an obvious issue of physical control. Curfews may be adjusted. Kids are more independent. They're developing new friendships and expanding their social circle. Parents are increasingly outside the loop as their teenagers carve out an independent social identity.

Parents also sense a loss of control emotionally. As children separate and form their own identities, they may rebel against their parents' cherished ideals and goals. Adolescence is when many kids have to be dragged kicking and screaming to houses of worship, avoid family functions, and drop out of activities they previously enjoyed. The child who used to rush home from school for a hug and a chat may now rush to his room, slam the door, and treat any questions about his day as an outrageous invasion of privacy. As one mother of a fifteen-year-old told me, "The single biggest thing I've learned since my daughter became a teenager is how stupid I am."

These changes in relationships with parents, friends, and teachers are normal, but that doesn't make them easy. Most children go through some rough patches in their teen years. But children who have been prodded and pruned and pushed, as so many today are, face very particular and demanding transitions.

Take Todd, for example, who came to see me at age fifteen because he stopped doing schoolwork, ignored curfews, and was possibly involved with drugs. An eager, willful boy, the eldest in a family of four sons, Todd was always a bit of a handful in school. Indulged at home, he had little structure or discipline in his life, but his parents, both professionals, had very high hopes for him. Diagnosed with ADHD in fourth grade, he nonetheless, with the help of tutors, managed to get generally good grades and even stay on the honor roll. Large physically, Todd was successful at sports and, again, had extra coaching in the sports that he did well in. At his parents' insistence, Todd took trombone lessons, too. In sixth grade, his parents struggled, against teacher recommendations, to get him admitted to various honors classes. Again, with tutoring, he managed to keep his head above water, although by the end of the first semester, he was forced to drop one of the honors courses.

Todd matured earlier than most of his friends and, as they continued to grow, he was no longer the largest boy in the class. His prowess at sports, which had depended largely on his size, evaporated, and, as his classes became more difficult, he was no longer able to maintain good grades in any honors classes. He no longer played hockey or basketball, and he refused to continue with his trombone.

By fifteen, Todd felt like a failure. He was finding little success in the various activities—academic, athletic, or extracurricular—that he was involved in. His parents could barely conceal their disappointment at his lack of success in both sports and schoolwork. Their efforts at coaching and tutoring him had convinced him that they only cared about his success. He was confused; he had no idea of what really interested him: He had only pursued those activities that pleased his parents and that would yield results in terms of immediate success, so he refused to do most everything. Though Todd would not initially admit it, he felt wildly out of control. He reacted with anger to his parents and teachers. Todd was so angry, in fact, that even if he had wanted to continue some of his prior interests, he now rejected them because of their association with his parents.

Todd is, in outline form, typical of the trajectory of pushed children. Successful in elementary school due primarily to their parents' focus and rewards, they never develop the imagination or the genuine internal sense of competence and motivation that they need to achieve real success as they grow older. Some, if not many, children can be pushed to succeed in their early years. But to succeed past middle childhood, drive and persistence must come from the child, not the parent. In many cases, imagination and motivation are more important to success than even raw talent. That's why it's more important to cultivate a child's drive than to push them to build a résumé. But ironically, building motivation in a child is a process that depends more on the child's inner desires combined with skillful parenting that focuses on character development instead of achievement.

What happens when a pushed child reaches adolescence? As one of my patients so succinctly put it, "It hits the fan!" Indeed, it often does. Many parents who have successfully engineered many aspects of their child's social, athletic, and educational life find that once their son or daughter arrives at puberty, their formerly compliant child slams on the brakes and the "success" train grinds to a halt. Sometimes, a child like Todd, who was pushed beyond his abilities, is forced to deal with his limitations for the first time at a more difficult time in his life, and without the resilience that other children have developed earlier. Other children, who perhaps are particularly talented or gifted, begin to question every aspect of their lives and their relationship with their parents, and decide that they are no longer willing to accept someone else's goals.

Pushed kids often experience very particular types of adolescence. Push parenting may result in a more defiant, confused, and difficult adolescent period, as a child refutes the parents' position and "acts out."

When parents have more philosophical goals for their child—goals that might include honesty, self-discipline, industry, good citizenship, etc.—children are freer to experiment and learn through trial and error what interests and pleases them. They gradually adopt their own specific personal goals. They also, usually, have learned to cope with failure and to see the world as a place where they have some control over the outcome of a situation. And they have come to accept responsibility for their actions, enjoy their successes, and learn from their failures. They simply have less to rebel against.

An adolescent is very busy developing autonomy. For any child, this can be a struggle. A pushed child has more difficulty finding out who he is—what really interests him, what gives him pleasure—because he has been so undermined, consciously or unconsciously, by parents who have been working hard to produce the child they want or need rather than the child they have. These pushed adolescents have a kind of partial identity formation. This incomplete identity will be a source of unhappiness as they struggle to become autonomous adults. Like houses built on sand, they lack the very things their parents would wish for them: solid identities and the strength to meet new challenges.

This isn't to say that adolescents don't need goals and a drive toward achievement. But, aside from the general expectation that they work hard in school, they need their *own* goals. What they need from parents is *structure*. I often use the analogy of a swimmer: An adolescent, like a swimmer, needs a wall to push against to do the best possible turn. Parents need to serve as a "wall" for their adolescents—a structure for them to push against as they move into the world to find themselves. Parents need to be around to set the limits and provide the structure.

As a child tests the waters beyond his family, he naturally looks for support elsewhere. Teachers and coaches can be important influences. But typically, the most significant cushion your child will have in the world in the teen years, outside of the family, is strong friendships. A major task of adolescence is forming a network of peer support. Teenagers want to be with their friends. When they're not physically with them, they want to talk with them on the phone or "instant message" them. This takes time, pure and simple. A pushed child—a child who is busy and directed in every free moment—simply doesn't have the time he needs to build the friendships that can cushion him through the bumpy ride that adolescence can be.

It's not only lack of time that prevents kids from forming crucial social webs: A spirit of competition fostered by parents can corrode the social atmosphere and force teens to behave more like lone wolves than the pack members they long to be. Parents who are always asking about other students' grades, activities, and accomplishments, always comparing their child to "the competition," create an "us against them" atmosphere in which teens become reluctant to share information. Many students find this tension escalates in the senior year of high school, when parents become secretive about college applications. "Don't tell Kevin you're applying to Amherst. The more kids applying from our high school, the worse your chances." This runs counter to teens' natural and appropriate inclinations, which are to share their thoughts, goals, and ambitions with friends.

Not only do parents' competitive attitudes isolate teens, they also serve to isolate parents themselves. Parenting a teen is difficult for anyone, and the task is made more difficult by the emotional and actual isolation of parents who cannot bolster one another and share triumphs and tragedies. Sometimes the simple busyness of everyday work and household responsibilities prevents parents from forming bonds. But sometimes parents make little effort to get to know the parents of their children's friends because they see no value in that sort of contact. Many schools try to promote parent meetings in which issues such as curfews and drug and alcohol prevention can be discussed. While these formal situations are useful, the most important interactions among parents are those made informally, at 7 P.M. on a Saturday night, when one parent feels comfortable about calling another and asking if anyone will be home for the "party" their child has just described. Discussing curfews, behavioral issues, and expectations can give parents the emotional leverage they need to deal with a child who claims that "everyone else's parents lets them!"

Without a firm sense of identity and the support of a healthy peer group, these pushed adolescents are often at risk for troubling behaviors. We are all too familiar with today's teen demons: tobacco and alcohol use, drug use, eating disorders, risky sexual behaviors, crime, depression, and suicide. Within this mix we now have to consider a factor that can amplify and exacerbate all of the above: the Internet.

We all are familiar with the image of the teen who "cybernates" for hours alone in his room. Is he doing homework? Or engrossed in pornography? Or deeply involved in a fringe-group chat room? Or is he playing violent and sexually explicit games? The truth is that the digital divide between most parents' computer expertise and that of their children insures that we usually don't know what they're doing, and we have virtually no way to find out. And, unfortunately, if they're quiet and busy, most parents are reluctant to "meddle."

It's particularly difficult to be an adolescent today. Many children are maturing physically faster than ever before. Various reasons have been proposed to explain this phenomenon: It could be related to better nutrition, to hormones in food products, or even to the increasing amount of light that children are exposed to in a postindustrial age. Whatever the cause, middle-school students who look, dress, and act like high school seniors are not uncommon.

Most children are eager to seem older than they are and will push for the signs and privileges of the next highest rung on the ladder. Many parents encourage this reaching upward by permitting behaviors and dress that are inappropriate. Unfortunately, today's fashion makes it particularly difficult for parents of girls to keep appearances in check. Skintight tops, bared midriffs, and Wonderbras all make it more of an uphill struggle for parents who fight the tide. A sixteen-year-old girl I saw as a patient had received a sexy bra and panty set from Victoria's Secret as a "sweet sixteen" gift from her girlfriends. Boys who adopt the ghetto fashion look, who are chatting on cell phones and checking their beepers, can have an air of sophistication that baffles their parents. It's very easy to forget that most of these kids are really sheep in wolves' clothing. Emotionally, they are children.

In my hospital work with children, we are accustomed to refer to a patient's mental age. This is because many of our children have brain injuries or diseases that affect their mental development. I think this is a useful approach when dealing with all children, particularly adolescents. A thirteen-year-old who looks like a twenty-year-old has the intellectual and emotional maturity of a *thirteen*-year-old. In our culture, children of this age are not prepared for sexual activity, for mind-altering drugs, for extreme violence in films and TV, or for handling social or familial roles that are really suited to adults. Unfortunately, too many adults take young teens at face value and expose them to situations that are inappropriate.

I know of a young girl (she was in fourth grade at the time) whose mother encouraged her to read *Memoirs of a Geisha*. The mother was reading the novel in her book club and was clearly thrilled that her daughter had picked it up and become engrossed. A beautifully nuanced story of the life of a geisha in turn-of-the-century Japan, the book, while not explicitly sexual in content, was nonetheless entirely inappropriate for a young girl. The mother's delight in what she saw as her daughter's "accomplishment" was entirely misguided. She felt that her daughter was exhibiting a clever precociousness. In fact, reading this sort of material, if not a waste of time, is more likely to confound, arouse, and disturb a child. A child, even a young teenager, will always enjoy the attention she earns by reading or doing something beyond her years, but the ultimate glean of the experience is at best marginal and at worst negative.

Too often, children, and particularly young adolescents, are burdened with information that they haven't yet had the experience or maturity to make sense of. Children need to be given the time to develop a level of abstraction, of conceptualization that will inevitably become increasingly sophisticated. You can't rush this process. Indeed, it's the process that counts.

Adolescents are making difficult and important choices every day about their lives. Should I do my homework or watch MTV? Should I write the paper myself or find one online to copy? Should I get home at curfew or sneak into a club with friends? Should I hang out with my old friends or try to break into the cool gang by smoking or using drugs with them?

These decisions will help determine many aspects of their future lives. It's extremely difficult for an adolescent who's been pushed to achieve and pushed to mature to make good, well-reasoned choices when faced with more immediate satisfactions at every turn. Too many young people have family relationships and moral frameworks that have been built on sand. When the crush of adolescence demands becomes overpowering, they are unable to make the hard choices that will lead to their long-term success and eventual happiness.

PART III

Solving the Perplexing Issues

Asking the Right Questions

Imagine for a moment that you, as an adult, must endure some of the trials of your children. You have a test tomorrow on community activities and politics. Then on Friday, you have a project due on household finances and a short speech to give on techniques for finding summer activities for your kids. You're not supposed to watch TV, even though you're exhausted and you'd like to, and, you almost forgot, someone is coming over tomorrow to inspect your house, with a particular focus on your closet-organizing skills. Oh, and that big paper on family nutrition is due in ten days, and you haven't been to the gym in so long that you're going to get in big trouble next time you show up. The people you live with always seem to be annoyed with you, and no one will forget how last week you left the damp clothes in the washer until they mildewed.

Whew! What a way to live: anxious and stressed, with little time to unwind. Worst of all, you have to be good at *everything* you do. This is the world of the typical child today. Busy, pressured, and stressed. We've looked at some reasons why our children are in this spot. Of course, much of it is because of us! We, the parents, are trying to make their world—certainly their future world—better. But, as I've seen with so many of my patients over the years, it would help to step back, perhaps, to look at how well things are working, and to examine some areas where most parents feel uncertain.

Ed Koch, New York's popular three-term mayor, used to roam the streets of the city, asking the citizens to assess his performance. "How'm I doin'?" he'd yell to the crowds. The people loved it. There was something so humble about anyone, particularly a politician, asking for a progress report. It's hard to take a look at our own progress, because it's hard to be objective about our children and our own style of parenting. But you can look at some concrete things that will be helpful.

I've mentioned my experiences with parents who, through the illness or injury of their child, have been forced to take a fresh look at their lives and put things in perspective. Suddenly the world tilts and everything looks different. Most of us have experienced these moments of clarity about our children. Perhaps when your ten-year-old, looking taller and surprisingly more mature, steps off the bus after a month at camp. Or when you arrive at the playground and, for the moment before she notices you, watch your four-year-old daughter helping a toddler who's fallen off the swing, dusting him off and patting his head. Maybe it's that moment when you glimpse your pre-teen in the rearview mirror, pale and nervous with anticipation, on his way to his first dance. Or perhaps you're in the back of the auditorium, invisible, watching your child rehearse a play with grace and confidence. These moments occur if we can but grab them and savor them. They tell us more about our children than any class rank or trophy ever will. They provide a fresh perspective of who our children are—their level of maturity, competencies, relative deficiencies, and vulnerabilities.

Beyond relying on moments of clarity, every now and again take a second look at your child. You don't have to do this in any formal, rigid way, of course, but remember that your child is always changing—he's probably a very different person from the one you knew last year. Sometimes we're amazed to see our two-year-old make a great developmental leap. We'd grown accustomed to his eighteen-month-old self. This is even more of an issue with older children. Our fifth-grader may have different social concerns and school issues than those that preoccupied her in fourth grade. If you're living with an outdated version of your child in your head, it will be harder for you to connect with him or her today.

LISTENING TO YOUR CHILD

Most of us just don't spend enough time with our children. Working parents are often stressed and exhausted at the end of the day. Even parents who work at home are so often distracted by multitasking that they have precious little downtime to just sit and listen, chop vegetables and listen, or fold laundry and listen. Actually, modern conveniences like the dishwasher can take their toll on parent-child conversations. No more drying while Mom washes and chats, or putting the dishes away while your brother washes and Dad dries. No one wishes to go back to a time when we all chatted by candlelight. But that quiet, relaxed conversation with our children can be hard to achieve. We must rely on more artificial "quality time" opportunities for listening. We want to have a meaningful conversation between 9 and 10 P.M. Perhaps we sit on their beds as we tuck them in, and expect them to spill the beans on what's new and what's bothering them. Or, after a frantic week of little contact with our children, we take them to lunch on Saturday and expect to "catch up" the way we might with an adult friend.

There are drawbacks to this style of listening to our children. One is "overlistening," where parents focus so intently on what their child has to say that it contributes to the "center of the universe" child. Over time, this kind of parental focus can encourage children to become self-centered and self-absorbed. The other problem with trying to listen on schedule is that it just doesn't work. Kids don't operate on schedule when it comes to sharing things that matter to them. We've all had the experience of tiptoeing out of our child's room at bedtime, turning to shut the door as he says, "Mom, why don't I have any friends?"; or when dropping them off in front of school, just before they jump out of the car, they confide, "My teacher really hates me." You must be prepared and available to seize these moments when possible.

There are two critical ingredients in effectively listening to your child. The first is time: There is no substitute for being there. You simply have to spend time with your child and give him opportunities to open up and share things. It's often better to focus on something other than the conversation, whether that's driving somewhere, doing a chore, or enjoying an activity together. It's similar to creating a diversion, a technique often used in therapy with school-age children. I may play chess or checkers while talking with a patient. As the child becomes comfortable, engrossed, he often lets his guard drop. But to take advantage of the distraction, you must be able to listen with attention. Sometimes this means turning off the radio in the car when you're chauffeuring your child to activities. Sometimes it's effective to ask your child to "keep you company" while you make dinner or walk the dog. The point is to create opportunities for relaxed conversation.

The second ingredient, one which parents often forget, is silence. Sometimes you just have to be quiet. That means not leaping in with advice or criticism the minute your child opens up to you. We've all had this experience as children. We finally worked up the courage to tell our parent that we were troubled about something, and before we got the words out of our mouths, Mom or Dad leaped in with advice about what we should do or criticism about what we should have done. Or offered pat advice like "It will all work out," which seemed to prove that they were not listening at all. Remember how that felt? Our children probably feel the same way. Of course, now we understand why our parents did it; we have an overpowering urge to do it, too. But sometimes your child simply wants understanding and support. If you are going to give advice, give it gently. Introducing a suggestion with "Have you thought of trying . . ." or "One way you could approach that situation might be . . ." is far more effective than a dogmatic "You must . . ." Giving advice this way not only encourages children to be more receptive to the information you're sharing, it also leaves the door open for your child to confide in you the next time around.

WHAT ARE YOU LISTENING FOR?

When a child comes to see me, I have a lot to learn. I usually have been told what the identified problem is—the child is refusing to go school, acts disruptively, or maybe seems sad. My job is to learn specific details about the child's life, many of which come from the parents. But I also need to learn about how the details are perceived. This is the critical aspect of my work, where training and experience come into play to help me distinguish between distortions and accurate descriptions. Without the perceptions, the details are of limited use.

Remember in the movie *Annie Hall* when both Diane Keaton and Woody Allen are shown in a split screen. Each is in a session with their respective analysts who ask, "How often do you have sex?" Diane Keaton replies, "All the time; three times a week," and Woody's response is "Almost never; three times a week." Facts, without perceptions, are not very helpful.

So when you listen to your child, you must consider the facts as well as your child's perceptions of them. For example, I had a child who told me (and this is not uncommon), "My teacher hates me." Now this ten-year-old boy was a good student, well behaved, and there was no obvious reason that the teacher would dislike him. When questioned, he told me that she had scowled at him on a few occasions and had called on him once when he didn't know the answer. He felt convinced that she had a very low opinion of him. When I investigated further, it turned out that the boy was extremely sensitive and also shy. His parents were soft-spoken, with gentle manners. The teacher by contrast tended to be stern and gruff. With the child's and parents' permission, I spoke with the teacher. It was clear that she favored him. The child had simply misread his teacher. It was his perception that was flawed.

Of course it's not just the child's perception that counts. It's the real-life context of that subjective experience that is going to give you information that's telling. If you don't know enough about your child's life—the ho-hum, day-to-day experiences and details—then you are at a distinct disadvantage when it comes to listening to him.

Here are some particulars you might pay attention to that will give context to your child's life:

- How does your child like to spend time at home? When she wants to relax, does she like to read, watch TV, or engage in imaginative play?

- Who does your child choose to play with? What type of children attracts him or her? Quiet, introspective children or boisterous, active ones?

- Does your child prefer to be with others or to play alone?

- What kind of book does your child prefer? Fantasy? Real-life stories or biographies? "Problem" books about family situations?

- What does your child think she's best at? Worst at?

- What's his favorite part of the day? Least favorite?

VARIATIONS

Kids are different. Having more than one will drive this fact home, as any parent of two or more will tell you. Kids differ in their biology. What's obvious is that they come in all sizes, shapes, and colors. What's less obvious is that they are equipped with five senses of varying degrees of acuity, sensitivity, and reactivity. Fine motor and gross motor skills may vary. Some youngsters may excel at intricate Lego projects (fine motor, visual spatial skills), but may struggle with music or dancing (gross motor, nonverbal skills). One child may be agile as a monkey, spending the day up in a tree, climbing and swinging, while another child prefers to sit under a tree or on a towel and read a book, play with a toy, or watch a bug. Yet another may paint and draw, sloppy and happy, while the next abhors texture or mess and prefers card games or chess. All of these children fall under the bell-shaped curve for normalcy.

Children's activity levels vary as well. Some children are up with the sun (or even before), playing and talking, while others can't be awakened with a cattle prod. Some are finicky eaters; others shovel it in with such haste that one wonders how they even taste their food. Some children are born with a sound and flexible internal clock: They settle easily into a routine. For them (and their lucky parents) naps and mealtimes are simple routines. Some children are rigid in their adherence to a schedule, and any change seems to set them into a nosedive. Take a plane trip and they are unsettled for the entire vacation. A missed nap calls for an exorcism. Even the introduction of a new food or article of clothing can set them off.

All children have a certain temperament—the style they use to handle what life dishes out. We refer to some youngsters' style as "easygoing," others' as "difficult" or "rigid." A large part of the role temperament plays in development is similar to what shock absorbers do for your car. Certain easygoing temperaments are like great shocks—the ride feels smoother, regardless of the terrain. Other more rigid, inflexible, or intense temperaments make for a bumpier journey, even when the way is paved with care. Children with more "rigid" temperaments are generally considered to be at a higher risk for developing other emotional problems. They have a hard time modulating their internal states and are often moody and demanding.

The distance traveled is identical, but the experiences of the journey differ.

Does your child wake up happy, ignore teasing, and persist at a task even though she doesn't succeed? Is she willing to try something new? Does she generally appear content and resilient?

Or does he wake up whining or cross? Does he find a stuck bureau drawer a personal insult? Does a stubbed toe set him off on a tantrum of screams and tears? If he spills his morning cereal, is it the end of the world and your fault to boot?

Parents who have the first type of child may find parenthood a relative breeze. They wonder at the struggles their friends describe. Parents of the second type can be driven to distraction as their child ricochets from one frenzy to the next. They can begin to walk on eggshells around these difficult youngsters so as not to "set them off"—a precursor to setting up unhealthy power struggles.

YOURS, MINE, AND OURS

"Look, the baby has your eyes." "There's no denying that baby has your stubborn willfulness." It's an unavoidable impulse: to identify traits your child has as "coming" from Mom or Dad or Gramps or Aunt Millie. It's natural to identify with your child in this way. But it's very important to remember that each child is unique, with his own specific traits. No one is a simple duplication of a parent, even though they may resemble one or both in many distinct ways.

It's not uncommon for a child to be brought to my office by his or her parents and, in the course of taking a history, I learn that little Johnny is "just like his dad, tearing around the house and constantly interrupting," or that the daughter is "bashful and shy, just like Mom." Rarely is the occasion of visiting my office a happy one, so generally the parents are less thrilled about the inheritance they're identifying than they would be of, say, big blue eyes or their incredible grace. But this kind of identification with a parent is often a tip-off to a possible struggle going on between the parents over who their child is. Thinly veiled animosity between spouses can be expressed in the way they see their child.

To see your child clearly, you have to step back from genetic stereotypes. Just because your daughter is shy doesn't mean that she will suffer the same social anxiety that you did, or that your very active boy, like his dad, will end up getting thrown out of secondary schools. This type of identification is different from the "mirror, mirror" identification described earlier in the book because it usually involves the opposite spouse pointing the finger. It forces the child to be a player in a less than happy marriage. It is absurd to divide up the traits of your child, sorting out and splicing together what came from where. That is not how genetics works. Of course children do inherit traits and tendencies, as well as specific characteristics, from their parents, but how those traits and tendencies play out is uncharted territory.

I hope that taking a second look at your child will help you to see her clearly as a special, unique person with her own skills and interests, strengths, and weaknesses. You can't really be an effective parent without a clear vision of your child. And you'll be less likely to push—or at least better able to resist the urge to push—when you recognize that your child must make her *own* future, just as you did.

Strategies

When I first undertook to write this book, I was reluctant to give any specific advice. As a psychiatrist working with children, I know too well that one size does not fit all. People tend to want generic answers to problems, but the truth is that such answers are not usually helpful. How could I give advice in a book that would be helpful to a broad range of people? Finally I realized that the best way to frame advice is the way I do it in my practice: I look at a particular problem and structure a response that's tailored to that unique situation. I think I can be more incisive and helpful by illuminating the particulars; you can then find the general themes that will be useful to your own unique family and situation.

In the questions and answers that follow, you may find some advice that is helpful to you and some that isn't pertinent at all. I've tried to include questions that are the most representative of those I get from patients. All of the situations and questions included are based on actual experiences I've had in my work, though all have been modified to protect the privacy of my patients. I hope that you will use these ideas as points of departure for your own discussions with your family and friends.

SCHOOL AND LEARNING STRATEGIES

Parents are understandably preoccupied with school and learning issues these days. Are our children doing well? Are they motivated? What is our role as parents in helping them learn? What about homework? How should we deal with teachers and schools? Does it ever make sense to let them fail?

Schoolwork is really our child's job, beginning in kindergarten. Children must learn to get along with others, work in a group, prioritize their tasks, and hand in assignments on time. It's not always easy to know when to step back to let a child learn something on his own and when to leap in and keep him from stumbling. And when is a learning style a learning disability? Here are some examples of the type of questions parents frequently ask about school and learning, and some particular suggestions on how to handle or at least think about certain situations.

Reading Readiness

My son is just finishing kindergarten, and I recently had a real shock. We went with a girl in his class to buy the teacher an end-of-the-year gift, and I gradually realized that my son's classmate was actually reading the greeting cards in the shop.

She knew every word. My son is bright and does fine in school. But he can't read a single word. I had no idea that they were doing more than learning their letters. I called another mom when I got home, and she claimed that her son couldn't really read either except for a word or two, but that she did know that some of the children in the class could read. As you might imagine, I was confused by this.

For the past few weeks, I've tried to work with my son on a computer program for beginning readers. He has no interest, and in fact is now struggling with me about spending any time on it at all. On the bright side, I found a class that my son can join for the summer that focuses on reading and writing skills. It's a six-week program and is fairly expensive, but I truly think it's worth it if it will give my son the advantage of going into first grade up to par with the other children. Don't you agree that the time and money spent now, while he's just beginning his school career, is worth it?

Kids learn to read at different rates. As long as your son is making progress and his teachers think he is doing fine, then it won't matter if he starts to read in kindergarten, first grade, or even early second grade.

Parents see reading as crucially important and of course it is. It is the main avenue for learning in all areas. But, like learning to walk, there are large differences in the rates at which children learn to read. Children who are early readers, moreover, are not necessarily better readers than those who learn to read later on. While some children are adept at grasping the basic skills needed for true reading by age five, many are not. Very early readers are of three general varieties.

The first category of early readers is children who are clever and receive a lot of exposure to reading. They learn to memorize whole words and recognize them on the page. They often memorize entire picture books and when to turn the page (this is especially true of youngsters who have listened to audio books that ring a little bell or have another such cue for proceeding to the next page). While these kids are reading in the sense that they are staring at the page and recognizing words, they have a fairly finite number of words that they actually can read. In addition, if handed new words, or "nonsense" words, sounds that can be pronounced but do not make true words ("words" you try to use in a tight spot in Scrabble), they are at a loss as to how to pronounce them. These are whole-word readers, and they still need to master the necessary phonological awareness and retrieval needed to become fluent readers of new material.

The second type are children who have remarkable verbal skills and an impressive vocabulary. They generally score in the high-to-superior range on standardized testing of verbal skills. However, the astute listener will find that their use of language is a bit off; these children miss the nuances of interpersonal communication and have abnormalities in the ways they speak. For example, they don't modulate the volume of their voice as well as others their age do. And they don't have the same musicality or fluid languge of their peers. In addition, these children may begin to read as early as age three or four. Mechanically, they have "broken the code"—they are able to "bust up words"—and yet they seldom "get" what they are reading. Their comprehension skills may be significantly delayed, not only in comparison to their reading skills, but also in comparison to their nonreading peers. These children are often referred to as "reading too soon."

The third and last type is a child who at a very early age has mastered the task of decoding. These children have learned the alphabet, discriminated which sounds go with which letters (and letter combinations), can put those sounds together to form words, sentences, paragraphs, and they're off! They generally master the technical aspects in conjunction with the content, so their comprehension is on a par with their reading skill (provided they are reading age-appropriate material).

Remember, too, that children's ages, and thus their developmental levels, can differ by almost eighteen months in a kindergarten class. There are large variations in the rate at which children of the same chronological age develop—all within the normal range and none signaling future success or failure. You'd never expect a six-month-old baby to walk. And whether a baby walks at eight months or sixteen months has no significance to his ultimate success, athletic or otherwise. Thus it is with reading.

Many children learn the technical process of breaking words down into their smallest bits (phonemes) and sounding them out long before they comprehend what they are reading. Other children are slower to "break the code," but are stronger in comprehension. Still others may be slower in both. As long as your son knows his letters and their sounds, has a good vocabulary, can recall words, and can identify the names of things, he will probably start reading on his own very soon. Sitting with him for long stretches, "working on reading" with flashcards and the like, may be boring for both of you and make him tired, annoyed, and angry. Reading books and words that have meaning to your child (even "Stop" signs and "Don't Walk" signals are of interest to the earliest reader) can be fun and "educational."

Sometimes putting too much pressure on a young child can actually have the opposite effect that you intend. You may find your son resenting the time he spends in reading class and deciding that learning isn't much fun after all. A child who looks at reading as a tedious chore is not well prepared for academic success. Your son will also probably figure out that you have a goal for him: learning to read. He may then become fearful of not meeting your expectations.

Here's what I suggest. First have a meeting with his teacher to reassure yourself that your son is making appropriate progress. As you say that your son is bright and doing well in school, there probably is no learning issue that you will have to deal with. Thus reassured, I think it would be wise to cancel the summer reading. Spend some time reading to your son for pleasure, perhaps at bedtime. Don't worry at all about whether he's "learning" from the experience. Don't try to "teach" him. At this point, it's more important that he come to appreciate that knowing how to read is a skill that can provide tremendous pleasure.

Report Cards and Homework

My third-grader just got a terrible report card. I had no idea he was doing so poorly. My husband and I are really upset and uncertain how to proceed. My husband wants to punish him by grounding him for a few weeks. He also thinks we should begin rewarding him for good grades so he has an incentive. A boy in his class gets a dollar for every A and it really seems to work. Do you think this is a good approach?

An unexpectedly bad report is always a shock. Ideally, parents have some idea of how their child is doing. But I think two principles are important to keep in mind when it comes to report cards: Reward effort, not results. Don't punish poor marks.

In your son's case, I think you have to focus on rewarding effort. First, you must understand what his teacher expects in terms of homework, and how your child is graded. You should be in touch with his teacher to find out what the expectations are and in what areas your son has been performing poorly.

Parents should have an overview early on of how much homework the teacher is assigning. Given the recommendation that children in elementary school should have about ten to fifteen minutes times their grade level in total homework time, your son in third grade should have about a half hour to three quarters of an hour of work each night. If the teacher is giving much more homework than that, or if your child is taking a longer time to complete it, this is something you should discuss with the teacher. Your job is to provide a quiet (no TV!) spot, paper, pencils, etc., and your general interest.

It's important to know your child: Some kids are exhausted after school and need a couple of hours to unwind; they work best after supper. Others are in "learning mode" and do well to finish their homework right after a snack and then have the evening free. I know one student who found, beginning in fourth grade, that getting up an hour early in the morning (he was an "early-to-bed" boy) worked perfectly for him. The house was quiet, and he did all his homework with an efficiency he never had in the evening.

If your son puts in a reasonable amount of time on his homework and still seems to be getting poor grades, then you need to learn, through a discussion with the teacher, if the assignments are too difficult for your child and how to help him. Some children with mild attention problems find it extremely hard to sit and work, even for relatively short periods of time. These children usually require a particularly quiet and secluded place to study. A cooking timer or other such gizmo helps them to work for ten minutes then take a three-minute break. If your child cannot focus or remain seated despite these interventions, don't assume that your child could do it if only he or she wanted to. Some expectations are incorrect for some children. It may be necessary to have your child evaluated more thoroughly.

Parents often wonder how they can reward effort. It depends on the child and their age. You need to keep rewards for learning in perspective. Parents often lose sight of the notion that learning should be its own reward. Some children respond to simple praise. If your son puts in his half hour and you simply tell him that he's done a good job, this may be enough. Some children might respond to extra attention: perhaps a board game after his homework. Some parents key TV watching to homework: When homework is finished, a certain amount of TV is allowed. This is OK if the child doesn't rush through homework to get to the TV.

Rewarding effort is one thing; paying for grades is another. Recently my daughter's public school sponsored a "leaping for dollars" campaign, where the children raised money for programs by jumping in place. While I willingly reached into my pocket to finance that endeavor, I would not encourage your husband's proposal for "learning for dollars." After a while, every time a book is cracked open you hear the faint cha-ching of a cash register. It adds up. And it doesn't work. Many research studies show that when rewards are the reinforcement for behavior, kids become more focused on the reward. Say you decide to pay your child one dollar for every book he reads, he will be inclined to start reading shorter and shorter books. If you try paying one dollar for every one hundred pages he reads, he will probably to start to skim.

If parents are obsessed with grades, children will be, too. Parents usually start to think about bribing their children for good grades in middle and high school. Elementary school kids usually don't need that kind of a carrot. Your praise and enthu-siasm is more than enough. But after years of excessive, unwar-ranted praise, or parents not being around enough to seem genuinely interested in them, kids become less responsive and more cynical. Parents reach into their pockets generally as a last resort, not a first. And kids appear to respond because they want the cash.

Rewards, under the right circumstances, are often effective. So it's not that bribes bother me—it's that grades cannot always be controlled. A child can work very hard and still miss out on the honor roll because of a quirky test question, a misunder-stood assignment, an illness, or, rarely, a punitive teacher. Most of this is entirely out of his or her control. If you want to re-ward your child, reward the *behavior,* not the theoretical out-come of that behavior (i.e., honor roll). This means that you'll need to know how much time and effort your child is putting into homework at night. You'll also want to have a dialogue with his or her teachers and review reports about your child's effort, attention, and diligence during the school day.

Maybe you and your husband could resolve your disagree-ment this way. If he wants to use money, OK, but reward the "effort honor roll," not the absolute grade-point average. This may be a more subjective, and time-consuming, endpoint, but by assessing the hours spent working at home and teacher com-ments, you can figure it out.

What about punishment? For study habits and, it is hoped, grades, proactive positive reinforcement used effectively obvi-ates the need for punishment. If you have outlined in advance (usually after a bad report card) what the teachers and your ex-pectations are, what the punishment (consequences) will be, and have done your part to help your child focus on his work, then a reasonable punishment can be appropriate. "Punishment" should generally be the result of not getting what would have been the reward, that is, missing out on the positive reinforcement. For younger children, this involves not getting to see *Scooby-Doo* or *Rugrats* after dinner. With older kids, not getting to go out with their friends, or not getting to use the car keys can be quite an incentive.

Kindergarten Curriculum/Jumping a Grade

My daughter is in kindergarten. She seems to be happy: The teacher is good and she is beginning to make friends. Certainly she's eager to go each day and talks a lot about the activities when school is over. But here's my concern: She went to a very academic preschool, and, in fact, is quite ahead of the children in her current class in terms of skills. I also worked with her at home, and she's quite comfortable with the alphabet and is beginning to read. But the curriculum of her school doesn't really expect them to read until first grade. She doesn't get any homework, and they mainly seem to play all day. Should I go to the teacher and see if it makes sense to move her up a grade? If the teacher discourages me, should I consider moving her to a private school that is more rigorous academically? Or should I consider working more with her and teaching her to read myself?

From the sound of your description and concerns, you have taken a front seat in your child's early education. She must be about five, perhaps four years old, if she recently started kindergarten. It is encouraging to learn that she knows her letters and is beginning to read. I can understand your delight in seeing her start down the path of what you hope will be a long and enriching educational journey.

Reading readiness in general is what is emphasized during the early kindergarten curriculum. So, given that this is the beginning of the school year, I can certainly understand why the teacher is neither sending home assignments, nor expecting the class to read.

Homework for "preschoolers" has become popular in many schools. Sometimes it is something age-appropriate, like bring in something from your home that is red. In kindergarten, assignments may evolve to include letter writing and sound (phoneme) recognition and writing. There is relatively little harm in these types of "assignments," and for the most part children like the idea of doing their "homework," especially if they have older siblings who get daily assignments. However, the parent who feels that their five-year-old isn't getting enough in the way of homework may be looking for more than is helpful.

Five-year-olds need to learn their letters and to solidify sound and symbol recognition, which in turn will help them "break the code" as they begin to read. Usually this occurs toward the end of kindergarten or the beginning of first grade. They also learn their numbers, and some begin to do simple addition and, less commonly, take-aways, using manipulatives. The clever teacher leaves them wanting more. Too much material or too many demands may leave the kindergarten child apprehensive, annoyed, or reluctant to pick up a book at the library or to play counting games. In addition, the classroom population may differ dramatically in their abilities, and the teacher has to gauge assignments to accommodate the whole range.

It sounds as if you and your daughter are happy with her current teacher. While your daughter says she just "plays" all day, the teacher may be teaching the class an enormous amount of material and just making it "fun." Your daughter wakes up eager to go to school. That counts for a lot. You should go and speak with the teacher about your concerns that your child is not receiving enough "academics." I imagine such a discussion would enlighten you about just how much work is being accomplished in the course of the day. If you have a child who is begging for more work, you can speak to the teacher about what she or he would recommend and then buy a workbook from which you can make your own assignments.

I would not recommend skipping a grade or transferring to a different school if your major reason for doing so is a more academic kindergarten. Your daughter has made a successful transition from preschool to kindergarten. Her academic journey is just about to begin. If she shifts into high gear before first grade, she may run out of gas before junior high.

Tutors

My sixth-grader is beginning French. He's finding it very difficult and has failed his first two tests. I'm thinking of getting a tutor. Does this make sense?

If a child is suddenly doing poorly in school, a parent quite naturally sees the poor grade as the problem. Too often, the first thought is to look for solutions to improve the grade. The common impulse is to want to call in a tutor or simply demand that the child work harder. But I think it's important to first take a step back and focus not on the grade but on the child. If you try to get a fuller appreciation of the total picture, you're more likely to come up with a solution that works in the short as well as the long term.

In your son's case, for example, here are some of the questions I would ask before I even began to think about a tutor. I would want to know what kind of student he is in general. Do things come easily to him, or does he have to work hard to achieve? Is he responsible about doing his homework independently, or does he need more supervision and encouragement? A new language makes particular demands on a student: Has he been doing his French homework consistently? Sometimes even a day or two missed can put him behind and make him feel frustrated. Was he eager to begin a new language or intimidated by the idea? What is his French teacher like? Is she very demanding? Do the other students have similar difficulty in the class? At times, a language requirement will mean a schedule change that could be difficult for the child. Is he missing out on a class that he preferred? Is French right before lunch, when normally he had homeroom and could snack on something?

If he is an excellent student and only poor in French, then the problem may actually be the quality of the French instruction. It may make sense to call a few other parents of students in his class to get a flavor of how his peers are doing. We all know that teaching methods vary; some teachers feel it's important to begin a course by being very demanding. If other students, on your son's general level of achievement, are also having difficulty, then it may make sense to schedule an appointment with the teacher to explore the situation.

If he is the only one having difficulty, and there is not some environmental explanation for it, then you need to consider whether your son has a more pervasive language problem. Students can manage for years to compensate for certain learning difficulties by being clever and adaptable, but a foreign language is a unique and demanding challenge. If your son has a more significant underlying language problem, he needs appropriate testing and remediation. A discussion with the teacher and appropriate school personnel should guide you here.

Finally, I think that tutors are too often relied upon as a crutch for students who actually need more focused study skills and more supervision of homework. While in appropriate situations a tutor can make a dramatic difference in a child's performance and confidence, when used at the first sign of a poor grade, the child begins to learn that he cannot learn on his own, that he must have help. I think it's important to explore other options before rushing to hire a tutor.

Working with Tutors

My son's high school just sent home a note to parents about tutors. It seems that many tutors are actually doing kids' homework instead of just giving guidance. My son's English tutor is supposed to be working with him on writing themes and that sort of thing, but to be honest, I'm not sure exactly how much my son does and how much the tutor does. Should I take a more active role in what goes on? I hate to interfere, because my son really likes his tutor and seems to be making good progress.

Tutors have become very common in middle- and upper-middle-class neighborhoods today. This is good and bad news. The bad news is that reliance on tutors takes the pressure off the teacher to teach material well and thoroughly. The tutor becomes the safety net: He will explain it later on, at home. Likewise, using a tutor takes the pressure off the student to attend and try to understand material in the context of the classroom. Why should they bother if they know it will be explained later on at home?

Moreover, tutors are not necessarily good teachers. Many do not have any credentials beyond their own education. Some people employ tutors who are only a few years older than the child being tutored. These young tutors are generally well-intentioned youngsters in need of some cash who have little or no experience teaching. They are most likely to end up doing homework for their clients, often without intending to or realizing that what they're doing damages a student's progress.

Hiring a tutor can exacerbate the "center of the universe" problem discussed earlier in the book. The tutored child may begin to feel that producing good work and learning is really something that someone else should do for him.

When you consider employing a tutor, you really have to think about what your child needs. Do they need a "homework buddy" who will simply help them focus? In that case, a very carefully supervised young person may fill the bill. But if your child needs help in actually learning the work, you need to consider the training of the tutor and precisely how they plan to work with your child. Your son should be able to write an outline alone, work on it with his tutor, write a draft alone, review it with his tutor, rewrite a final draft, and hand that in to his teacher.

If your son needs help "learning to learn," then he may benefit from a remediator. Remediators work on skills. They address the underlying difficulties or weaknesses that some students may have with basic language, retrieval, organization, and study skills. Homework assignments may be used as a vehicle for these skills, "a point of departure," but most effective remediation is not based on homework.

Whatever your son requires in the way of a tutor, it's important for you as parents to understand what work is being covered and how, and that the tutor understands the role he or she should be filling.

Should My Child Be Tested?

My son is in kindergarten and so far it's been a disaster. The teacher says he won't stay in his seat. He disrupts the class. He doesn't seem to be making any friends (this is his fifth week of school) and he certainly isn't happy. A friend says that he might have learning problems, and that's why he's acting out. He seems fine and happy at home, and I've never noticed anything about him that would make me think he has a learning problem. My husband thinks he's just adjusting and needs a few more weeks of school. But I'm getting worried that he may go from bad to worse and get to hate school so much that I won't even be able to get him to go. It's already becoming a struggle in the morning. Do you think I should have him tested? Do you have any other suggestions that would make him like school?

From your description, it sounds like your kindergartener has gotten off to a rocky start. This may be due to a number of reasons which should be assessed before you have your child "tested."

To begin, I would want to know what sort of preschool experiences, if any, your child has had. For the youngster who has been at home for four years of life, going off to a foreign place, with relative strangers in charge and a new routine, is an enormous change. On the other hand, if your boy has been attending day care and/or nursery school and is fortunate enough to have a few kids in his kindergarten class who are familiar faces from his preschool experiences, I would expect the transition to kindergarten to be relatively smooth.

Does your son have difficulty separating from you? Is his schedule different from previous years? Is he, for instance, in the afternoon program, when normally he'd nap? Or are you rushed in the morning, when dropping him off, so you don't miss your train to work? Relatively minor changes in routine can result in dramatic behavioral changes in young children.

The teacher's remarks that "he won't stay in his seat" make me wonder how the classroom is structured. If your teacher requests that the children remain seated for ten- to twenty-minute intervals while doing a project (as is the case in most kindergarten classes) that is quite different from a child who cannot remain in his seat for thirty minutes listening to a "lesson." The latter is, in general, not to be expected of a five-year-old; the former most kindergarteners can handle.

Transportation to and from school is also an often-overlooked piece of the puzzle when trying to understand what's contributing to school problems. If you drive or walk your child to school, then this factor is probably less important. But if your child takes the bus, you need to know how that's going. Is he happy on the bus? Does he feel safe? Young children who are bused with older students are often frightened by the noise level and baseline chaos on the school bus. Occasionally an older kid may outright threaten or intimidate a child. I had an eight-year-old boy as a patient who was a very bright and popular youngster in his class, but out of the blue developed numerous complaints of headaches and stomachaches. After a while it became clear that the symptoms were exacerbated Sunday evening and remitted Friday afternoon. Though it was obvious the problem was school-related, his teachers had no idea what was causing the difficulty. On closer evaluation, it turned out that two older boys were tormenting the child on the school bus. He did not want to tell on these boys because they had threatened retaliation if he did.

I would certainly sit down with your son's teachers and ask

them to share their impressions with you in more detail. If the teachers have had years of experience, and you feel they may have a fairly accurate perspective on your child, then I would ask their opinion about an evaluation. Sometimes just a clear statement of the classroom expectations, boosted by some small tangible reward (e.g., sticker, ice cream) will produce positive results. If, on the other hand, the classroom expectations are unreasonable, you may need to discuss this with the teacher and, if necessary, the principal.

Lastly, just because your child has never seemed to have "learning problems" at home doesn't mean he wouldn't have "learning problems" in the classroom. Many children are fine in a one-on-one scenario that makes minimal demands on them. Especially if this is your oldest child, it is hard to gauge what is "normal" and what is less than normal within the confines of home and family life. If your teacher, with experience, feels your son is demonstrating persistent and significant difficulties, or if you feel that there is nothing you can do after assessing what I have described above, then by all means have him tested.

You shouldn't be concerned about how your child will feel about the testing itself. Children like being "tested"; they get the individual attention of a professional with expertise in working with children. They do standardized tests that assess an array of neurodevelopmental functions, all the while thinking they are "playing games." Most kids are sad when it's over and ask to come back. My only reservation in testing a child immediately is that we don't want to miss other aspects of his experience (routines, classroom expectation, transportation) that are negatively impacting his adjustment.

Unhappy with Teacher

My fourth-grade daughter's teacher really doesn't seem to like her. She grades her papers very harshly. She's always gotten A's before but now she's getting primarily B's with an occasional C. I've heard other parents complaining about this teacher, as she's known to be tough. We're only one month into the term, and I think my daughter is getting discouraged. I wonder if I should speak with the teacher about it, or perhaps complain to the principal.

Things that adults pick up on are not necessarily critical for making or breaking an elementary school experience. The teacher who appears to blow you off may be the very ticket for a fantastic educational year. Their priorities are, and should be, the kids, not the parents.

For one thing, the beginning of the year is usually fairly chaotic, and it would be unwise to jump to conclusions too soon. Give your child and her teacher time to warm up and get used to one another. See what happens. If after six to eight weeks you still have reason to think that the teacher is rejecting or disliking your child, make an appointment. Bring your partner. Leave it open-ended, without a specific agenda, saying you just want an opportunity to hear how she feels things have been going with your daughter. Listen to the teacher's comments. Are her words consistent with her actions? Does she appear to know your child? If the discussion feels productive, you might want to share concerns that you worried that "they hadn't gotten off to the right start," and work toward establishing a mutual understanding and dialogue. You may learn something new about how your child behaves in school.

Remember, not every teacher is going to be the perfect fit for your child, nor the creative enthusiast embodied in that Mary Poppins of academia, Ms. Frizzle. Every teacher does not have to *love* our kids in order to teach them. Most effective and inspirational teachers do love what they do. And it's great when a teacher and student hit it off, when we feel a sense of love between them, but it's not a necessary part of learning. It *is* necessary that a child respects her teacher, and in turn feels that she is respected and treated fairly. Believe it or not, good lessons often come out of not being the teacher's pet.

Despite what you've heard from other mothers about this teacher, do your best to work proactively with her. Try volunteering as a helper on school trips, in the lunchroom or library. Make yourself useful. This may reassure you that horrible things are not happening in the classroom while it attenuates whatever difficulties you see existing between your child and this teacher.

If you feel that the teacher is extremely hostile or defensive, you may want to speak with other parents (to learn their experiences from previous years and this year's class). I generally recommend speaking to the principal only in crises (such as violations of safety or ethics) or for chronic problems that have not resolved with parent-teacher intervention. This serves two purposes: It reserves the principal for higher-level issues, which is not only an appropriate but a more effective use of his time, and it avoids getting the parent labeled as a complainer and troublemaker by going directly to the principal. It's always a bad idea to alienate the teacher and school by calling for preferential treatment. In these instances, you use up chips you may wish you'd saved to cash in at a later and perhaps more critical time in your child's education.

Homework: Motivation and Procrastination

I am really, really tired of having to be so involved with my child's homework. I am about to give up. I just can't come up with any more ideas to make my sixth-grade son do his work himself. He procrastinates until the very last minute, and I wind up hounding him constantly and typing papers for him with gritted teeth. He's bright and when he does buckle down, he does fine, but this year he seems to have lost all motivation. I'm at my wits' end. Do you have any suggestions?

Getting older kids to sit down and do their homework can be quite a challenge. Here are a few general suggestions.

What time of day does your son get home? What is he doing after school? Some kids do not get home until 7 or even 8 P.M. They have sports practice, music lessons, religious school, tutors, and so on. By the time they eat and flop on the couch, it's bedtime. Instead, they turn to homework with half an eye closed. If your son has a routine like this, I'd recommend taking a look at what you can change. You can't pack it all in, it just doesn't fit.

Next, I would definitely stop typing his papers. Unless the teacher has asked you to do this because your child has graphomotor difficulties, there is no reason for you to be typing. Even if your teacher did condone your contribution, I would suggest you teach your son to type himself. I say this for a couple of reasons. First, it is very unusual for parents to be able to limit themselves to the role of a stenographer. You may have all the good intentions in the world, but as you transcribe the fractured grammar, misspelling, and relatively disjointed prose of your twelve-year-old, your adult brain will begin to change it. Maybe not the first time, or the second, but gradually, inevitably, you'll find yourself dusting and polishing his prose.

First the spelling, then grammar, until finally you're rewriting their work. I can say for certain that if an adult repeated sixth grade at this time in their life, they would do quite well in expository writing (at least with regard to class rank). But you do not need to repeat sixth grade, and your son is the one who needs to learn from his own mistakes. No matter how "instructive" you may be with your corrections, the lessons learned are yours more than his. He needs to do his own work, be accountable for his part, and own his failure and success. This won't happen if you are typing his papers. In six or seven years, he should be away at college, and, unless you planned on boarding alongside your son, he's not going to have you around to help him. Best that he learns how to swim now, before he's out in the deep end, alone.

Next, you raise the question about motivation. What motivates a child to learn changes as he matures. Pleasing parents and teachers in elementary school begins to lose its appeal in middle school and becomes downright uncool and nerdy for some students in high school.

How and what are his peers doing? Do other mothers complain of similar problems? If he's not doing his homework at night, what is he doing? "Chatting" on the Internet? Hanging out with friends watching TV? MTV? Are you concerned that he's getting involved with drugs? Sometimes a change or loss of motivation in schoolwork is one of the earliest signs of personal problems including social rejection, anxiety, depression, or substance abuse.

It is rare for bona fide learning disabilities to first present in the teen years, but occasionally a very bright child can compensate for significant deficits in some neurodevelopmental areas for many years, only to start to have serious problems later on. In middle school there are often changes, including new and larger high school buildings, lockers for books, changing school schedules. These changes can present quite a problem to teenagers who have organizational weaknesses. They begin to feel overwhelmed, worried, and have secondary problems caused by an impaired capacity to concentrate fully on school, class assignments, and homework. You might discuss with his teachers how they perceive his work and his study habits. This should give you a good basis on which to proceed.

ADHD: Confidentiality and Medications

My third-grader has been diagnosed with ADHD. He has been on the medication for a week and seems to be doing well. Here is my question: I'm wondering if I need to tell the school that he has been diagnosed and is on meds. I'm not sure that there's any reason for them to know, and I'm afraid that he'll be stigmatized in some way and maybe it would even affect his friendships if word got out. What do you think?

I can understand your reservations regarding your child's diagnosis and treatment. In addition to your concerns about stigmatizing your child, there are very real issues related to privacy when schools are informed of medical conditions. But in general, a child whose learning style or behavior warrants medication has already been earmarked by the faculty as a child with problems. Seldom are teachers surprised when a parent informs them that a student is on medication for Attention Deficit Hyperactivity Disorder. In fact, unless your child recently started at a new school, teachers should have been consulted as a resource in arriving at the diagnosis.

Most teachers are appreciative and respectful of the confidential nature of this type of information. It is important that we rally together as adults on behalf of a child to help maximize the therapeutic benefit of this intervention. To leave the teacher out of this equation is to begin a collusion with your child regarding his treatment. It sends powerful messages to your child about whom he can trust and what he should and should not let be known about himself. It also implies that there is something shameful about his learning difficulty. All of these are potentially negative experiences.

In addition, there is the final and important fact that your child is on a medication that has side effects, including cardiovascular changes, and the school nurse should be aware of this in order to best care for your child in the event of an illness, injury, or drug reaction. Without the knowledge of what medication your child is taking, medical care could be compromised.

Is My C Student Learning Disabled?

My fifteen-year-old son is generally a C student with an occasional B. He's never been particularly active and is a kind of daydreamer type. I had him tested to see if there's any real reason for his poor marks and inattention. The doctor said he has some features of "ADHD inattentive type." I asked him about medication, and he said that he didn't think it was warranted. We thought that medications were always indicated with any type of ADHD, and I wonder if we should be taking him to another doctor for another round of testing. What do you think?

This question raises some very difficult issues that probably boil down to individual preferences as well as medical acumen. I personally and professionally do not agree with using medication to "improve" an already adequate performance. I think medication should be used to treat pathology. To me a C is not pathology. When I was growing up a C was average, a D below average, and an F was failing. Nowadays, a C is not felt to be good enough. But I would consider that your child may be suffering from the vanity sizing of the "Almost Perfect" kids . . . That is, B's are made into A's, but C's are not necessarily made into B's.

I also wouldn't treat a "daydreamer" type just because he's dreamily looking out the window. Some questions I would be inclined to ask are: Does he often forget his assignments? Does he fail to complete things he starts? Does he lose his homework a lot? Are you doing most of his work for him, so that these C's would be F's without your input? If you answered yes to the above questions, then perhaps another evaluation is warranted. But if you answered no, then leave your boy alone. He may not be the greatest student right now, but that doesn't mean he's headed for failure.

Good Grades, Lazy Student

My twelve-year-old son is a good student and has always been on the honor roll. I have no real complaints about him except this: He rushes through his homework and, though his grades are good, I think they could be much better. When I ask him if he's done his work, he always says yes, and then he watches TV or plays video games. If he were failing or doing poorly, I'd feel I could limit his time spent this way. But is it legitimate to limit his TV and video time if he's doing OK in school? And should I be more demanding that he do his best rather than just get by (which is a phrase he's heard from me a million times to no effect)?

It sounds to me that your son is a bright child who has developed the ability to complete his work independently. The fact that he is on the honor roll is reassuring, though criteria for inclusion vary dramatically among schools. I suggest you speak with your son's teachers to learn whether or not they are pleased with his work. Most experienced teachers are aware of who is working hard and who is taking it easy. What is the quality of the work your son is handing in? If your son is handing in work replete with careless errors, then you have a bone to pick regarding his hasty jobs. If, however, it is carefully completed and thoughtful, you don't. Find out how much homework the teacher thinks he is assigning. If there is a truly large discrepancy between the two, then perhaps your son needs some additional, more challenging assignments. Ask the teacher about this.

Your child is first and foremost a twelve-year-old boy, and has at least six more years of high school ahead of him. He should be able to hang out with friends, play ball, and relax. He needs to do his work, but he shouldn't be penalized for doing it relatively quickly.

At the same time, you need no excuse for setting a limit on TV and video game time. In fact, I routinely recommend that every home have a restriction on what and how much TV viewing and electronic gaming goes on. If you allot a specific amount of time that your son may watch shows or play Nintendo, rather than insisting that he finish his homework before he can play, you may find an answer to the first part of your question. Your son may be rushing through his work because the sooner he finishes, the earlier he starts watching or gaming and the longer he can play. If he were allowed only an hour of TV, whenever he wanted, he would have to pick and choose what he watched (a good exercise in prioritizing) and would not feel the pressure to get through his assignments, since no amount of hurry will expand his TV time.

SOCIAL AND APPEARANCE ISSUES

How a child functions in the social world is important. Most of us derive great satisfaction from our interactions with other people. Moreover, good social skills are important for success in any arena from the workplace to the home. But there's a wide range of social temperaments in children. Some are outgoing, while others are shy and reclusive. You won't change your child's underlying social template, but by understanding and respecting his temperament, you can help him navigate through the social issues that he'll face as he moves from the nursery through the treacherous shoals of middle and high school.

Many teachers feel that simple social skills—the ability to share, respect for others' property, knowing to wait your turn—are as important to success in the early school years as any skill or ability connected with academic learning. Sometimes, in their effort to "improve" their children academically, parents forget the significance of interpersonal skills.

Physical appearances are also always important—to our children and to us. Adolescents, in particular, suffer agonies about how they look, and usually resent anything they perceive as parental interference. It's always a delicate balance between imposing matters of taste and giving thoughtful and respectful guidance. At times, the best technique for dealing with teen appearances is five years of biting your tongue. But when it comes to health-related weight issues, parents sometimes must become involved. In any event, parents must be the first line of defense against a culture that places far too much importance on certain types of appearances. A balanced message about what matters and what doesn't has to begin when a child is young. It's very difficult, particularly when interacting with young girls, to curb comments about appearance. "Oh, what a pretty girl!" is often our first comment when seeing the toddler in her delightful dress. But I think it's important to try to steer away from such comments, particularly as girls get older. Reacting to a girl's behavior, rather than her appearance, is really more constructive.

Of course, there's another aspect of "appearances" that preoccupies us in connection with our children. "How will it look?" "How will they look?" It's natural to want our children to shine, to do well, to look good. But sometimes we cross the line. Today it's difficult to know where the line *is*. Looking at other parents' experiences and questions helps us to focus on issues that are common to us all.

Here is a sampling of the kinds of questions parents ask about these areas of concern:

Winning at What Cost?

My daughter, a high school junior, is a candidate for student council president. From what she says, it looks like she has a reasonably good chance of winning. We've helped her make posters, and my husband had some great ideas for e-mails she could send to her classmates promoting her campaign. The election means a great deal to her and to us: She has a mild learning disability and ADHD, and is on Ritalin. She's never been a superstudent. So being student council president could mean a lot to her future (and, of course, to her self-esteem). The only remaining hurdle is the speech. She has to give a campaign speech in front of the entire high school. She's not a great public speaker primarily because she gets extremely nervous. We were talking about this at dinner, and she mentioned a drug you can take if you're really nervous. She heard about it from a classmate who used it for a college interview. She wondered if she could take it before her speech. At first I said no—it seemed a little crazy. But the more I thought about it, the more sense it made. After all, she would only use it once. And she already takes Ritalin (which she knows is supposed to help her performance), so it's hard to argue that you shouldn't take a medication for that purpose. It could make a big difference in her speech, the election, and her future. What do you think?

You are not the first parent to ask this question. Perhaps because public speaking is generally accepted as the most terrifying activity anyone can imagine, it's not surprising that we all look for help. And because we've become used to relying on medications for help in so many areas of our lives—for emotional as well as health-related challenges—it's not surprising that you would think that this drug could be the solution to your daughter's nervousness.

The critical issues here, however, are maturity, meeting challenges, and learning to succeed and fail by our own efforts. These are critical lessons, and ones that should never be subverted for any "gain."

It is absolutely normal that your daughter is nervous about public speaking. Her nervousness is the rule, not the exception. She has been challenged by learning differences and attention problems, and she sees this election as yet another challenge, an exciting one at that. But a couple of questions come to mind.

Children with attention deficit disorder, and some learning disabilities, often have a difficult time reading social cues. Is her assessment of this situation fairly accurate? Is she "in the running" for this political position? Or is she "clueless" about the realistic outcome of this vote? It is important to support her enthusiasm and aspirations, but also a parents' responsibility to help realistically gauge the circumstances.

Like so many children today, your daughter has grown up

taking medication daily. She may have gone through a period of defiance, when she was opposed to swallowing pills and said she would not continue Ritalin. But the very fact that you tell me she is a high school student and taking Ritalin means that she must acknowledge that on some level the medication has helped, made school more manageable, and enabled her to do better. Her request for a medication to help her a bit further seems like a logical next step. What is important to keep in mind, however, is that children who are treated with psycho-stimulant medications like Ritalin have significant problems with attention, impulsivity, and, often, hyperactivity. Without the medication, they are at a distinct and unfair disadvantage as compared to their peers. The symptoms are often covert, and, if correctly treated, usually undetectable. So a child, and their family, may forget over time that there were distinct and real indications for initiating medication. But indeed the Ritalin has "leveled the playing field" for your daughter; it has not given her an "advantage."

But in this situation, the pressure of public speaking, there is no pathology to treat. The child is "normal"; it is our expectations that are distorted. Treatments that enhance already normal functioning fall into the category of "cosmetic psychopharmacology." Do we want to teach our children to turn to a pill to upgrade their already normal performance? In this instance, you might reassure yourself as a parent that the medication to enhance performance would be taken "just this once," but I think it is likely that a child would turn to this medication to allay anxieties in other social scenarios as well.

A CEO or concert musician may indeed use a medication for their critical speeches or performances. The difference is that they are adults who experienced childhood public speaking and performing without drugs. Now their livelihood requires public speaking or piano playing and, for whatever personal reasons, they choose to take medication occasionally. Children and teenagers are not adults. Their bodies and emotions are still growing. They need to learn to rely on themselves, to try out scary things, and, if they "make a fool of themselves," to see that the world does not come to an end. And they certainly do not need their parents to take everything so seriously that they justify a child's nightmare that maybe everything *will* fall apart if they don't succeed.

Quite possibly your daughter's intense need to do well is in part driven by an underlying feeling that her effort has not been good enough. Despite your good intentions, the extra help you and your spouse have given her may in fact have served to fuel this perception. All your work may be sending her other messages: that this election is extremely important, that it will be terrible if she loses, and that there is no way she could do this on her own. As a child who is familiar with the routine use of medication, and feeling as though she could not handle this on her own, medication appears a reasonable alternative. On a clinical note, her problems with ADHD, and impulsivity in particular, may also make it hard for her not to want to be the best, and to achieve things quickly. These tendencies have probably contributed in part to her past mediocre academic achievement.

Finally, there are other, more appropriate ways to learn to feel comfortable speaking in public. Practicing her speech over and over again, with family for the audience, helps. You should certainly encourage her to do this. She might even find that taping her speech and listening to it herself would be a useful exercise. If she had sufficient time, she could join a debate team or even see a behavioral therapist. These last approaches would take an investment and effort over time, and the results would be gradual. But your daughter would own them.

Cosmetic Surgery for Son?

This may seem like an odd question: My son who is fifteen has a large nose. It doesn't seem to bother him—at least he's never mentioned it—but I've been wondering if I should suggest that he consider a nose job. I do think that a smaller nose would dramatically enhance his appearance, and he's at the age where he's interested in girls and his looks are important to him. I know that many girls get a nose job at around this age, and I wonder if there's a "window" of optimum timing for the procedure. Should I make the suggestion to him?

There's no doubt that cosmetic surgery is becoming more common among teens. Rhinoplasty, or a nose job, is the most popular cosmetic procedure among the under-eighteen-year-old crowd, according to the American Society of Plastic Surgery. Approximately one out of every ten nose jobs is performed on a teenager. Many plastic surgeons may perform a rhinoplasty on girls as young as thirteen or fourteen and on boys by fifteen or sixteen, if it appears they have completed their growth spurt by that time.

While it may make medical sense for a child to have a nose job performed during his or her teenage years, it presents serious questions and ethical concerns. Many if not most teens are incapable of making rational and balanced decisions regarding plastic surgery. They may know the right answers to give in order to get past the surgeon, but I doubt that they truly grasp the "bottom line." Few adults do. A rhinoplasty will change the size and shape of your nose. It will not necessarily make you popular, give you self-confidence, improve your self-esteem, career, love life, etc. And while adolescent after adolescent may nod their head in agreement to these words, deep down inside the majority believes, on some level, that this change will have larger, more profound, consequences. So do adults.

It sounds as though you may be more preoccupied with your child's nose than he is. If he hasn't said anything to you about it, I doubt that this is an issue troubling him. If you are concerned that he is more worried over his appearance than he lets on, try bringing up the subject by pointing out someone who has recently had a rhinoplasty.

I have no doubt that it would be a serious mistake to broach the subject to him if he hasn't initiated the conversation. I say this for several reasons. It's like asking someone who is quite content with what they're wearing, "Do you really plan to wear that to the party?" Of course, you can't change out of your nose as quickly. It may be a big blow to his self-esteem for him to think that even his mother thinks his nose is too big. We are all meant to be "beautiful" in the eyes of our parents. Even when what we see is an aesthetic three on a scale of from zero to ten, we should keep our misgivings to ourselves. A youngster, even a teenager, may be inclined to succumb to another's opinion of their looks rather than their own. Your boy might go ahead and agree to a rhinoplasty, only to regret it five or ten years from now.

In fact, the American Society of Plastic Surgeons has outlined three factors that predict positive outcome following adolescent rhinoplasty: The teenager must initiate the request, they must have realistic goals, and they must be sufficiently mature. If your son has a reasonably active social life, a handful of friends, and is willing to meet the world without holding his hand in front of his face, I would leave this issue of plastic surgery alone.

Toddler Socialization

I'm really worried about my two-year-old daughter. My husband and I both work and don't get to spend as much time with her as we'd like. The problem is that she doesn't seem to have any interest in socialization. In general, she's a great kid: very lively and responsive. Her nanny takes her to the park most every day and says she is happy to play by herself. If another child approaches her, she'll smile, but she never gets involved in sustained play with someone else. The worst is, when my husband or I take her to Gymboree on the weekend, she seems to hate it. She cries and clings to us and refuses to sing or engage in any group activity. We've been trying to arrange more playdates for her on weekends, but they're usually disasters, as she goes her own way and leaves me and the other mom or nanny to struggle to arrange at least some parallel play. Those situations are really embarrassing. We've also signed her up for a toddler dance class to get her used to other children, but we haven't seen any positive results from that thus far.

Two-year-olds normally vary a great deal in their degree of "socialization."

Socialization begins when a fetus hears its mother's voice in utero; it continues throughout life. The fact alone that your toddler is not "actively social" is not worrisome. Your child appears to fall toward the "shy" and "slow to warm up" side of the spectrum. During the week, with a low-pressure routine at a nearby park that she shares with her (hopefully) familiar nanny, she may be more relaxed and open to new experiences. From what you say, she smiles at park playmates, though has little interest in sustained play. She is making eye contact and not avoiding other children, which is positive because gaze aversion and social avoidance may be markers for more serious socialization issues.

A weekend at home with parents who both have a heavy workweek tends to get jam-packed with "errands and enrichment." Your child does not sound like the type who can just pick up and go, and the trepidation she experiences with transitions mushrooms when she realizes your urgency and anxiety about her reluctance to perform like the "other children." It doesn't sound like you and your child are getting any enjoyment out of the process.

Parents are led to believe that children, even infants, need orchestrated opportunities to become well-adjusted, interactive people. This is a piece of developmental disinformation. I remember reading an article from a popular parenting magazine while I was waiting to see the obstetrician. The article described six-month-old infants going on playdates. These babies reportedly relished one another's company and were saddened when the playdate was over. Even the author, who portrayed these opportunities as really positive experiences for the infants, felt duty-bound to add a disclaimer that the playdates were not necessary for normal social development. The vast majority of toddlers, in fact, become capable social animals despite our interventions, not because of them.

Your daughter is only two. Gymboree programs and Mommy and Me are as much, if not more, for the parent as the child, and definitely not necessary for healthy development in the end. The importance of social skills comes center stage when a child begins school, and the world of their peers eclipses home life. Of course you should expose your daughter to other children on a regular, casual basis. Visits to the park, family gatherings, and encounters with other mothers with children your daughter's age will all help her learn about other people in her world.

And beware, a two-year-old is often in a power struggle with internal drives, particularly as they pertain to toilet training. If these children start to feel that they are being forced into doing activities that they do not want to do, they tend to dig their heels in deeper, becoming stubborn and defiant.

Capes and Costumes

My five-year-old son is really into Batman. He's seen all the movies and watches the cartoon all the time. He's even asked me to call him Batman. My husband pretends to make him fly all the time and he really enjoys it. My problem is that he insists on wearing a towel pinned to his shirt as a cape. I don't have any problem with this, and I've let him wear it to school. The difficulty is that the teacher has asked that he not wear it. Frankly, I don't see that it should be an issue, and I think it probably makes his adjustment to school easier. How do you think I should handle this?

Most of us can remember a time in our own childhood, or that of our siblings, cousins, or nieces/nephews, when imaginary friends were constant companions. I know of a darling five-year-old who had two, Custard and Maria Catcha, who "lived" with her and her family for close to a year (foreign exchange students?). It is an enchanting and transient stage of development, where the mix of fantasy, autonomy, and control get played out with colorful imagination. Kids get us to do things for their imaginary friends that they know they probably shouldn't, wouldn't, couldn't get done for themselves. "The friends" have to have a place set at the table. Would you please change the channel? "They" don't like this show. "They" need the middle seat in the car. Sorry, but "they" need a PB&J instead of grilled cheese for lunch.

The majority of youngsters go through a period of identifying with a superhero, boys more so than girls, but with the Powerpuff Girls saving the world before bedtime, this may change. Your son is not unique in his absorption with Batman. And it is not uncommon for four- and five-year-olds to demand to be called by their superhero name. They wear Batman underwear and sneakers, carry Batman knapsacks, and eat Batman-shaped pasta in their Batman bowls in front of Batman cartoons. In fact, there would be no end to the Batman shtick if it were up to your son and the commercial world. But I am certain there are times when you say no.

As you say your son is five years old, I assume that he is in kindergarten. Getting started in kindergarten is a big deal, and I can understand your concern that the transition be made as easy as possible. But I respect the request of the teacher that the "cape" stay at home. Part of going to school is realizing that you are one of several children in a class, and you are there to learn. It is *Johnny* who is in school, not Batman. While fantasy is fun and often educational, the teacher does not want it imported into her classroom. Though this may seem cold and bureaucratic to you, it is an important lesson and central to school.

Think about it from a more practical perspective. If the teacher permitted your son to wear a cape, surely some other children will begin to think that a costume is just the ticket for school. Suddenly you have twenty-four five-year-olds flying around the room in what would come to resemble a production of the *Rocky Horror Picture Show*.

When it comes to these kinds of issues—what's appropriate and what's not—a parent must simply take a stand and insist that a child conform to the rules, as tempting as it may be to try to get the rules to bend. Your child will have to respect authority on many occasions in life. This could be the beginning of his learning that, like it or not, he must sometimes accept a decision that comes from above.

Compromising

I feel almost ashamed to be asking this question, but I don't know anyone I can talk to about this. My son is in seventh grade. He's a bright boy and really an absolutely delightful kid. The problem is that next year he will be applying to a competitive private school. His grades are good but not extraordinary. He plays tennis but he's not a top-notch player. He doesn't play a musical instrument, and he's never held a class office. The bottom line is that he doesn't really have any qualifications to make him stand out from the pack. He is a good writer and does have some creative flair in that area. So here's my question: There is a writing contest I read about for kids in his age group. He'd have to write an essay on the person he most admires. I thought that doing well in something like that could really help his application. I mentioned it to my son, but he's not interested in entering. My impulse is to demand that he do it, with my help and that of my husband, who is an advertising copywriter. I've actually thought of writing the essay myself, just making him read it and change it if he wants. I feel confident that we could produce something that would win at least third place.

I realize that doing this is a little out of bounds. On the other hand, this is the way the world works, and if he gets into this school, it could make a big difference in his future. Do you think there is any downside to us helping him in this way?

It is truly quite tempting when you believe you have the ability to make a big and immediate difference in your child's life by doing what for you would be a relative no-brainer. You can almost hear Satan on your shoulder: Write an essay for your son, have him make a few changes, and hand it in as his own. It would certainly have a good chance of gaining recognition, winning some prize, getting the A. As a parent, doing for your child is the easiest way to "feel helpful" and to express your love. (Actually, paying someone to do for them is probably easier still.) It is harder but infinitely more beneficial not to do for your child. Just as it was hard to see them toddle with an unsteady step, to wait patiently for what felt like an eternity as they tied their shoes (too loosely), or to watch them up at bat when bases are loaded and there are two outs in the ninth.

You rationalize that this may be the "break" that your child needs to gain deserved attention in school. It could "really turn things around" for him. I doubt it. The good and bad news is that *there is rarely a single event that significantly alters a student's trajectory toward success or failure.* Certainly, you could write an excellent paper, and your son could edit it, and make it seem like an authentic, if extraordinary, seventh-grade production. But in the end, that alone would probably not make much difference in his academic future. At least not in the positive way you assume. Even if he were admitted to the school, would he be able to compete with the other, perhaps more aggressively academic, students? Would he feel that he deserves to be there, or would he feel that he had deceived the admissions people in order to get in? Ultimately, in perhaps subtle ways, his sense of confidence would probably be affected. To say nothing of his sense of his parent as an honest, responsible figure, worthy of respect, and even, perhaps, admiration. It's difficult enough to maintain a strong bond with a child who is entering adolescence. A child who sees a parent cheat or deceive can be affected more deeply by it than you might guess.

When a parent knowingly colludes with a child to deceive a teacher or other authority, serious fallout occurs. Unless it is entirely in jest, the lesson a child takes home from this is that the end justifies the means. Win at any cost. Sometimes parents fool themselves by thinking, or even telling their child, "I'll do this for you just once, but never again." In most cases, the child didn't ask for the help in the first place, and to the child it can feel like the parent is shifting responsibility for the "cheating" onto the child.

The parent is setting the precedent here. The child is learning to deceive and to accept deception as the norm. It may seem like "what's the big deal," but it's just such a child who has difficulty understanding why it's wrong to buy a term paper on the Internet, plagiarize, or even get involved in shady financial dealings later in life.

Daughter's Unrealistic Weight Goal

My daughter is twelve and suddenly seems obsessed about her weight and her body. She is average in height and weight. She's about five foot and weighs around 115 pounds. She also seems to be right in the middle in terms of development. She has friends who are already quite busty, and others who show no sign of breasts. She is beginning to develop and has just bought her first bra. The problem is that she's decided that she's too fat. She suddenly won't eat much of anything. Or I should say she won't eat much at meals. I find occasional junk food wrappers in her room. I don't know how much to make of this. Obviously I can't force her to eat. She doesn't listen to me when I tell her that she's fine the way she is. Do you have any suggestions on how I should handle this?

Your daughter is not alone in her preoccupation with dieting. Studies have shown that approximately 45 percent of girls between the third and fifth grades (ages eight to ten) want to be thinner, and 40 percent have tried to lose weight. By sixth grade those numbers jump to a whopping 80 percent and 60 percent respectively. And 50 percent of all girls ages eleven to eighteen who have dieted report doing so with their mother's encouragement, according to a study in the *Journal of the American Academy of Child and Adolescent Psychiatry*. This same study looked at the prevalence of partial eating disorders in a nonreferred (taken from school or community populations as opposed to clinical ones) sample of high school girls and found that over 30 percent had features of anorexia nervosa or bulimia.

One can hardly be shocked that young women learn to be unhappy with their bodies. The media is saturated with images of unnaturally thin models, and fat is definitely out. For a child who is still in the throes of puberty, like your daughter, weight gain is the norm. In fact, some youngsters weigh more as they enter puberty than they do at its completion.

At 5 feet tall and 115 pounds, your daughter is within normal limits for the growth charts. However, using Kate Moss as her ideal, she probably feels obscenely overweight. It sounds to me as though your daughter is probably about to start getting her period, if she hasn't already done so. This is often an exciting but also somewhat scary experience for girls, no matter how sophisticated and mature they may seem. Trying to lose weight or stay small is sometimes felt to be a way that girls control their development. And indeed, if a girl loses a lot of weight, or fails to gain weight as she grows, her period will be delayed by months and occasionally years. It is also fairly routine for girls to put on extra weight in the months immediately prior to the onset of menses. This may be a helpful bit of information to share with your daughter, as she may be concerned that she is starting to gain weight for no clear reason.

The previously mentioned study in the *Journal of the American Academy of Child and Adolescent Psychiatry,* which looked at the relationship between dieting and calorie intake in preadolescent and adolescent girls, found that preadolescent girl "dieters" ate essentially the same number of calories daily as girls who did not identify themselves as dieting. Therefore, though your daughter may claim to be dieting, given the junk food wrappers you find in her room, her calorie intake may be no different than if she were not.

The challenge here is to avoid a power struggle. It sounds as if your daughter is already struggling with herself over her weight. The fact that she is skipping meals only to horde candies and junk food that she eats in her room suggests that her own self-inflicted efforts at dietary restrictions are not as effective as she might hope. Excessive preoccupation with eating behaviors within the family has been recognized as a risk factor for developing an eating disorder. Girls who begin to lose weight are infamous for their capacity to minimize the health risks and negative aspects of dieting. Butting heads with her over how you think she looks won't work and may undermine your ability to communicate.

I would start by trying to talk about weight as an issue for girls and women. You can point out that while Americans are on the obese side, dieting has become epidemic among teenage girls. The next time you are watching TV together, or in a doctor's office looking through a trendy magazine, point out the models or ballet dancers and what they really do to stay that thin. Talk about their constant dieting and exercise, their meager and nutritionally unbalanced meals, the high rates of substance abuse and hospitalization. It may help to comment on how unrealistic the images are. A good exercise is to walk through a department store and look at all the models in advertisements for makeup, cologne, clothing, and the like, and then look at the shoppers and the sales personnel. Do these groups share a great deal in common? The answer is almost always no. It puts into relief the contrast between how advertising makes us want to think of ourselves and how we truly are.

I would also be curious to know if any of her friends are currently dieting or have recently lost a significant amount of weight. Among teens, dieting is akin to an infectious disease and must be handled along the lines of a public health issue. Parents, especially mothers, need to talk. Perhaps some of her peers have mothers who are instigating this trend.

Finally, I suggest that you help your daughter "reframe" her desire to lose weight into a wish to "get in shape." Help her get into an exercise routine, maybe join along with her (she'll let you know if she doesn't want you to!) on a jog or some sit-ups. As you do this, you can also point out that truly healthy women are strong women. There are plenty of excellent young female athlete role models in this regard, from Marion Jones to the Williams sisters to Mia Hamm. If your daughter takes this bait, then an interest in nutrition might naturally follow. Keep healthy foods in the house, and encourage her to learn what the body needs to burn fat and build muscle.

I think you will find this approach more effective than telling your daughter she isn't overweight when she believes that she is. It is similar to martial arts: Use the momentum she has accrued to send her off in a better and healthier direction.

Son's Weight Gain

I'm having a problem with my son. He's fifteen and really a great kid. He does fine in school and has plenty of friends.

> *But, a year or so ago, he began to put on weight. I think it was because he used to play more sports, but now has gotten interested in music, so he isn't as active as he used to be. My husband is overweight, and I've really had to struggle to keep myself in shape, so it's especially hard to watch him get pudgy. Right now he's about five foot seven and one hundred sixty-five pounds. I'd say he's about ten or fifteen pounds overweight. I've spoken to him many times about cutting back on junk foods. I've tried to make nutritious meals. We even gave him some sessions with a personal trainer for his birthday. Nothing seems to work. I'm thinking of sending him to a diet camp this summer. What do you think?*

I can understand your concern about your son's weight, given that you and your husband both have had to struggle to stay in shape. As Americans we are too sedentary and heavy for our own good. We prefer to drive rather than to walk, to watch rather than to play, to grab some fast food rather than to cook and sit down to a leisurely meal. And it sounds as if your son may be developing some unhealthy habits. From what you describe, he does sound a bit on the chunky side, but then again, at five foot seven, I would bet he's due for a growth spurt soon. Some children grow "out" before they grow "up": Their weight gain is a preamble to a rapid increase in their height.

Your son seems like a popular and successful teen. If this is accurate, then I doubt that his weight is a result of social problems, feelings of peer rejection, or displaced desires or impulses. Its roots are probably in genetics, sedentary lifestyle, and growth patterns. I think it would be a mistake to send your son to a diet camp unless he is begging you to do so. This would label your son as having a problem that I am not convinced that he has. Fortunately for your son, boys are at much lower risk for developing eating disorders than girls. With the exception of sports like wrestling and diving, there is much less pressure on males to maintain a specific phenotype.

Here's what I would recommend: Since both you and your husband have struggled with weight, get rid of the processed and high-fat foods in your home. Once in a blue moon you all can indulge, but if you have to get in the car and run down to the shop to buy a treat, it's a premeditated ordeal. Forget about the personal trainer. At your son's age what he needs most is a basic understanding of his nutritional requirements and the skills to read a food label.

It may be best to have a nutritionist, preferably someone young, whom your son can relate to, teach him these points. Next, leave him alone. Right now he's on the fence. If your son has a TV or computer in his room, take them out. Limit his time watching television or online, and make him get out of the house each and every day. Perhaps you live within walking distance of a shop. Send him on errands to pick up something for supper or to deliver a package to the post office.

Depending on your relationship with your child, it may be helpful to share your concerns with him in an open and candid fashion. In particular, his father may be able to reflect on his own experience with obesity during his youth; some youngsters would be receptive to this type of discussion at age fifteen, others would not. You be the judge. He may or may not have a weight problem when he gets older. But any forceful effort on your part to control which way the scale swings now is likely to backfire on you in the future.

SPORTS

Sports have become a consuming issue for today's parents. What used to be just a fun activity, at least until high school, has now become virtually "professionalized" with high-stakes competition and serious coaching. Many parents have come to see athletic achievement as yet another notch in the belt or slot on the résumé. In their effort to produce a "well-rounded" child, they force their children into activities that they might not enjoy or even be suited for. This often backfires. Did you know that of the 20 million children who participate in sports programs outside school in this country, roughly 60 percent quit by age thirteen? The reason most children cite is that "it's not fun." Conversely, other parents worry about the pressure of sports on their children and how to handle it. To take the long view is difficult, given all the pressures that push children into competitive athletics. But it's important for parents to be realistic about the role of sports in a child's life, and also in the life of a family.

Flagging Enthusiasm

My ten-year-old daughter began swimming on a team this past year. She's doing incredibly well: The coach is telling me she's "a natural." My husband and I are thrilled about this. Our son is not athletic at all, and my husband, a serious athlete, has always yearned to see one of his children succeed at sports. We've signed my daughter up for extra coaching, and I'm exploring a swim camp that's reputed to be one of the best in the country. With the coach's help, we've begun to schedule meets that offer a higher level of competition than what our local clubs provide. And we're beginning to realize that this skill could be my daughter's admission ticket to a terrific college—the coach has already mentioned schools where he has contacts and which have strong swim teams. The problem is this: My daughter, who has seemed to really enjoy swimming up to now, is occasionally flagging in her enthusiasm. Of course, she's quite young, and doesn't understand the role that

*swimming could play in her life if she's successful. We've had
an occasional struggle when she's wanted to go to a sleepover
or birthday party that conflicts with a swim meet. We're sure
that these conflicts will occur over the years; we know that it's
hard for a child her age to maintain her focus. But we also
know that some children do manage to do so. And the truth
is, when our daughter wins a meet or does extremely well,
which happens frequently, she's absolutely elated. So here is
our question: How can we help her realize the importance of
her swimming to her future? The coach, who is working with
her on this, has suggested that we might consider a "motivational" coach for her. He's seen them do wonders for keeping
kids on track. We'd prefer to handle it ourselves, if possible. We
know there must be some techniques that can help young people maintain their focus, enthusiasm, and mental toughness
when it comes to sports. Do you have any suggestions?*

Nothing is like the heady feeling of watching your child excel
at any activity. Suddenly, you begin to see your daughter with
the gold medals around her neck and the college scholarship
in hand. This is perfectly natural. But too often parents get carried away, by pressure from coaches, with fantasies of future
achievement, and even by pressure from their own children to
leap into a premature commitment. Such parents may become
too invested in their child's achievement in sports.

While the dream of a college scholarship drives many parents
to think that sports will be the key to their child's future success, and all efforts at encouragement are therefore in the child's
best interest, there are real downsides to this notion. For one
thing, it's very important to remember that, when you're speaking of a young child—and your daughter is only ten—you're
looking at roughly eight years of single-minded commitment.

Your daughter is at an age when it's important that she experiment and try a variety of activities. This may be the only time in her life that she has the luxury to do this kind of experimenting. You must also be realistic and recognize that the chances that your child will gain a scholarship nearly eight years from now are quite slim; her body will change and her competition will become increasingly skilled and intense. Remember too that scholarships for sports are a mixed bag: Children who earn them have often sacrificed a great deal to win them and then face the pressure to perform in two arenas—sports and academics. The normal "slump" that athletes and students experience from time to time may, for a scholarship student, result in terrific pressure and anxiety. Moreover, depending on the type of student that your daughter is, and where she goes to college, a sports scholarship can actually undermine her self-esteem. She may be regarded as simply a jock at a school that makes greater academic demands than she's prepared to meet.

I always recommend that parents go slowly. Don't allow yourself to get carried away by the thrill of the initial success. Swimming will be there next semester and the one after that. You have to realize early on that the odds of your child becoming a first-rate competitive swimmer are small. So the effort and time and commitment you make to the sport should really be motivated *by your child's love of the sport* and your sensible assessment of how it fits into her life—not the other way around. By trying to encourage your ten-year-old daughter to miss birthdays and overnights with friends, you are trying to fit her life into the sport. First and foremost, she is a ten-year-old, and needs to be doing what ten-year-olds do. If she is truly driven to swim, swim, swim, then you can support her. If, however, you find that you are prodding her more and more to keep motivated, you need to reconsider.

I agree with your hesitation in hiring a motivational coach. Parents give up their authority too soon and too easily in the hopes of raising a superstar. There are many serious downsides to giving up parental control and allowing any type of coach to play an increasingly parental role. This does not mean that a parent should be breathing down the back of a coach during practice: quite the contrary. The parent should feel comfortable enough to be able to drop the child off and pick the child up, especially at your daughter's age. But swimming should be a *part* of her life, not her life. Her coach should be simply an athletic coach and not another parent.

I think you need to step back as parents and assess your situation. First, you have to have a serious conversation with your daughter. Is she really interested in swimming? Enough to give it a greater time commitment? Keep in mind that if she likes her coach and is being encouraged, she may well express more enthusiasm than she actually feels. This is perfectly natural and good; a skilled coach can be a terrific mentor for a child. That relationship can be worth encouraging. On the other hand, you are the adult and the parent, and must weigh your daughter's level of enthusiasm and perseverance. It's not uncommon for a child to leap into a sport with a parent's spirited encouragement, only to find that she's bitten off more than she can chew. The experience ends in disappointment, and the child sometimes feels that she's failed her parents and her coach, as well as herself, by not sticking with it and achieving success. Remember that at ten years old, she is at an age when she should experiment with a variety of sports and activities; sometimes committing wholeheartedly to just one can be a mistake.

A critical issue is time. You must carefully consider your daughter's academic demands. I always believe that schoolwork should come first. Sixth grade can require significant amounts of homework. Children who swim competitively are generally exhausted and need to sleep at the end of the day. They can't stay up studying for tomorrow's math quiz. Is your daughter the kind of student who can get her homework done efficiently?

Remember that a serious commitment to one sport can have an effect on other aspects of a child's life. She may have to turn down playdates and other activities. Is she truly willing to do this, and is it sensible for her to do so? Developing social skills is an important part of your child's maturation process. Having said all this, it may be that swimming will be your child's great love. You can give her the opportunity to discover this by going slowly. Maybe she can begin by having just one extra coaching session a week. You can discuss with her the fact that this is a trial period of, say, four months. If after that time period, she continues to love the sport and enjoy the work, and continues to do well in school, then you can consider increasing her commitment. This arrangement gives her an out as well. If she changes her mind, after the trial period she can gracefully move on without feeling like she's disappointed you and her coach. The important thing to remember with children and competitive sports is that the sport, and the related success or failure, should be *theirs*, not yours. What most parents don't see when they watch young people who are extraordinary athletes is that in nine out of ten cases, it was the athlete's determination, not the parents pushing, that made them a success. For example, Tiger Woods used to beg his father to let him golf. If your daughter really loves swimming, the impetus to go forward should always be hers, not yours. Your responsibility is to keep the broader picture in mind, to apply brakes when necessary, to support her when difficulties arise, and to applaud her success from the sidelines.

Sibling Comparisons

My daughter, Cindy, is a junior in high school. She's an incredible softball player. She's worked at it ever since fourth grade, and her father and I have totally supported her. She's had private coaching, pitching camp every summer, and we've driven her, it seems, halfway around the country for games. It's all paying off now: She's being heavily recruited by many colleges, and it's really exciting for her and for us. Every day we get e-mails and letters from schools selling themselves to us. The problem is my son, who is two years younger. He's a freshman in the same public high school and a great kid, but he's certainly no athlete. We encouraged him at every step, but he just has no interest. I guess we were a little disappointed in this as he is our only son. Here's the issue: The other day I heard him on the phone tell a friend, "They don't really love me anyhow. Cindy's the star in this house." He said it in a kidding voice, but I was truly shocked. Maybe he really does see things this way. I know we've been very focused on Cindy for the past couple of years, but I'm horrified to think that he would say we don't love him. I don't know whether to bring it up with him, or if I should just do something to make him understand that we love him very much.

I think it is generally important to be as honest as possible with a child, provided you remain within developmentally appropriate limits. By this I mean it is correct to tell a four-year-old that their grandparent has died, and bring them to the funeral. It is incorrect to discuss every detail of the demise, no matter how many precocious questions they may ask. I think parents need to stop and really think about what they overhear their child say. Don't immediately rush in and do a "guilt dump" by confronting them about how devastated you are that they could think or say that. After some reflection and conversation that includes your spouse, sit down with your son, tell him what you overheard, how you felt, and what you thought about it. Perhaps it is only your son's perception of the situation, not the reality. In that case, discussion and allowing the boy to express himself would be helpful. If his feelings are based in reality, you should count yourselves lucky to have heard his words. You need to seriously rethink the consequences of your present family dynamics. Do you make a point of always attending Cindy's activities while being too busy to be involved in your son's? Are you in touch with what your son is doing in school and with friends? Sometimes parents become so involved in one child's success that other children become second best, and they quickly pick up on this dynamic. In fact, this can happen when one child receives an undue amount of attention regardless of the reason, be it achievement, behavioral problems, or, as I described in the "Pushed-Apart Family" chapter, illness. It's one thing to say you love your son and care about him, but have your actions shown that to be true? Maybe the overheard conversation will stimulate some changes in your home that will benefit everyone.

Coaches

I've always thought my daughter's gymnastics coach is a great woman: She's enthusiastic and supportive, and I think the girls learn a lot from her about life. But I am beginning to wonder . . . My daughter is one of her best performers—she's nine years old—and I feel that the coach is pushing her too hard. My daughter seems worried about her weight. She's getting anxious about practices. And last week she started to cry when she learned that she had to skip practice to go to a fam-

ily religious ceremony. I've asked my daughter if she wants to
continue with gymnastics, and she insists that she does. I'm
not sure how to handle this.

Elite sports like gymnastics, figure skating, and ballet are
known for the pressure and stress they impose on athletes and
their families. It is not uncommon for the children who excel
in these sports to develop particularly intense relationships with
their coaches. Parents may even feel in competition with
coaches for control over their children. Coaches frequently
complain that parents refuse to leave the ice, gym, or stage and
let them teach. And while the majority of coaches are wise
and careful trainers, you are right to be concerned about your
daughter.

Coaches are judged on their pupil's success. Like the other
elite sports, appearance and weight are emphasized from an
early age. The rate of eating disorders and amenorrhea (abnor-
mal menstruation) among female gymnasts, skaters, and ballet
dancers is much higher than among other athletes. Even if your
daughter states that her coach is not encouraging her to diet,
she may be pressured to do so in subtle ways. Older teammates
may talk to her about keeping her weight down. At nine, she
must eat well and she needs to grow. In addition, as she becomes increasingly proficient in gymnastics, the demands esca-
late: physically on her body, socially on her time, and mentally
on her capacity for sacrifice and concentration. It may be too
much.

Despite her tears, you need to provide some balance in her
life. Discuss your concerns with her. Make certain she understands that she can slow down now and pick up the pace further down the road. If she is adamant about maintaining her
level of involvement in the sport, you should discuss your con-

cerns with the coach. The coach should recognize the potential for burnout, and work with your daughter to manage her stress. Lastly, if her apprehension builds and the routine hasn't changed, I would consult with a pediatric sports psychologist. These are professionals who have experience and expertise in helping manage the pressures secondary to elite competition.

Team Travel?

My daughter's soccer coach is organizing a trip to Italy for the whole team. The idea is that they'd be matched against Italian kids in a series of games for ten days this summer. Most of the other parents are very enthusiastic about this. The kids (who are ten) are excited too, but I'm a little nervous about the trip. My husband thinks it's a great opportunity, but neither he nor I would be able to make the trip due to finances and work commitments. I hate to have her miss out on a great experience—so far beyond anything I could have done as a child—but I still feel uneasy about it and I'm not even sure why. Should I let her go?

I think you must listen to your intuition. The trip could be a great opportunity for your daughter, or it could be a disaster. There's no doubt that going abroad is a wonderful and educational opportunity. Traveling and staying in a foreign country and experiencing a foreign language adds enormously to an individual's appreciation of the world and how they fit into it. But in this situation it may or may not be the right thing.

Here are some of the potential negatives:

Your daughter is young to be separated by an ocean from her home and family without a family member to cushion her adjustment. It's not just that you'll be apart, but also that she'll be out of a familiar context. Never underestimate the power of home for a child: It's not just the place; it's the food, the people, and the habits that help keep children on an even keel. In Italy, she'll have to adjust to things like a different language, different customs (dinners at 9 P.M.), different foods, and even a different bed.

I would also wonder, if finances are an issue for the family, why you would commit a large sum for this "experience" for your daughter when the whole family might benefit more from a closer-to-home vacation that includes everyone. I really think that these kinds of trips have more to do with what a parent wants or needs rather than what a child desires. The enthusiasm of the parents sometimes may overpower a cold, hard look at what the point of the trip is.

If you have an enormously soccer-driven child who is very independent—frequently and easily sleeps over at others' houses, has been on a plane, is very close with at least one member (preferably a mother) of the traveling group—and you have the money to devote to the trip, then it probably would be fine. But if you have questions about how your daughter would handle the distance and the separation, then I'd say you should hold off.

You might, by the way, find that your daughter insists she wants to go despite any misgivings she has in her heart. It's difficult to swim upstream when everyone else seems excited about the trip. But she may secretly be grateful if you insist that she has to wait another year before considering such a trip.

I once had an eight-year-old in my office who had been taken to Japan and Nepal by her parents. All she talked about was the disappointing lack of peanut butter-and-jelly sandwiches in those parts of the world. Yes, she saw the wonders of the Orient and the cultural diversity, and her horizons were larger following her journey, but I doubt that she gleaned from the experience half of what she would have if she'd been twice as old.

Reluctant Athletes

My third-grade son has no interest in athletics. His brother and sister are very active and involved in a number of sports, some at a highly competitive level. But it seems that no matter what our middle son tries, it's not for him. My husband and I both think that the experience of team sports is important for young boys but we've had no luck forcing him to join various teams. Should we give up?

This sounds like the old "You can sign me up but I won't go" syndrome.

Nowadays, sports have become something we watch our kids do. Increasingly extracurricular athletics are an area for *adult* competition. We have created a mini-Major League in our baseball program, with some "Little Leaguers" practicing twelve months a year just to keep their edge. Some soccer teams involve time commitments that impact significantly on a child's academic and social life. Ice hockey, with its costly and bulky equipment and the scarcity of "ice-time," ends up involving the entire family—skaters and nonskaters alike. (I know one mother who told her son he could not play ice hockey because there was no more closet space.) With all eyes and focus on them, some kids eagerly step up to the plate for love of the game, or love of the attention, or even fear of loss of love from the parents.

But not all kids are comfortable with this scenario. Some would rather play racketball at night or capture the flag. Your child may not be a joiner, may have poor coordination, or just not like being watched. Organized after-school sports are so saturated with competition that we've lost sight of the most important point of the game—fun, healthy exercise, camaraderie, learning how to lose, and celebrating wins.

Try to assess your child's physical and emotional inclinations in terms of athletics. Is your child shy, with poor hand-eye coordination or muscle tone? Then baseball and basketball are probably not for him. See if he enjoys swimming, or perhaps karate. During the elementary school years a child should be exposed to as much variety as possible. If your child continues to hold back at an age when most peers are actively involved, then you may want to say that your child needs to do one sport (i.e., a once-a-week activity) but he can choose which one. Set a limit on how long he must stick with it—three months? six months?—in advance.

If you think your child may be hanging back because of the social challenges (i.e., shyness) rather than the athletic ones, you may want to encourage less competitive interactions. Again, swimming is a good choice, and some team sports like soccer tend not to isolate one player in the spotlight (as baseball does) and are less physically demanding than is hockey. Not all children shine when placed in a highly focused performance-oriented activity. Sports that are less goal-oriented, like swimming, skiing, and gymnastics, among others, may be preferable for many children.

COLLEGE: THE END OF THE RAINBOW?

For many parents today, the final grade on their parenting is the college their child is admitted to. Harvard, Princeton, and Stanford equal an A. Middlebury, Georgetown, and the University of Chicago might be a B. State U would certainly be a C. Some parents are so determined to get that sticker for their rear window that they're willing to sacrifice their child's happiness, their relationship with that child, and even their own best instincts as parents.

We all know what's going on: the expensive SAT tutors, the gray area of who actually writes the application essay, the fudging of extracurricular accomplishments, the strings pulled to insure the right internship or research opportunity, and so on, and so on, and so on. I hasten to say that I am not a college counselor, and I have no expertise in advising students or parents on college selections. But I have seen how the cloud of the college application process has overshadowed many young people's adolescence and dominated their parents' concerns in recent years. I have treated many young people who have struggled with exaggerated parental expectations, and I've seen what this struggle has done to their maturation process, their sense of self, and their relationship with their parents and peers.

Coping with Rejection

My son is a high school senior. He is ranked number one in his class of about 250 at an excellent private school. He has been very successful in debate—won numerous trophies—and has excellent recommendations from all his teachers. His guidance counselor encouraged him to apply to some very competitive colleges. He applied to one early decision last fall and was rejected. He applied to four other top schools and was rejected from them all including the school his father graduated from. He is now on the wait list at what was supposed to be his "safety" school. To be honest, an Ivy League diploma has never been a real goal of my husband, my son, or me. But he certainly seemed like an excellent candidate and his school encouraged his applications. In this process, once you indicate interest in a school—and remember that my son's stats are very impressive—they inundate you with material and seem very eager to have you as an applicant. His hopes were built up at every turn. Now we have to live with the fallout. He's simply devastated. I don't have any real concerns about my son's abilities or future success. But I am furious at this process and am wondering what I can do to bolster his confidence. He seems so desolate and is finding it difficult to focus on school, and to feel optimistic about the future.

My question is how do I handle this with my son? How do I explain to him that just because he was rejected, he's still an excellent student, a worthy person, and that his future is bright?

You are not the first parent who has found the college application process stressful, dehumanizing, and demoralizing for you and your child. At least you have not made it the primary goal of your child's life, as many parents do. I think the most helpful way to deal with your son's quite reasonable reaction to this experience is to explain to him in some detail how the process works today, and how it is that intelligent, hardworking, and committed students don't always wind up at the college of their choice.

First, as you already know, parents must approach the college application process, and help their children approach it, in an informed and sensible way. Even well-meaning parents can find, as you did, a dispirited and demoralized child on their hands if they do not understand the way the game is played today.

I know that some parents will not be dissuaded, no matter what I or anyone else says, from pushing their child to Ivy acceptance at any cost. I've tried in the first two sections of this book to address the ultimately damaging effects that this kind of inappropriate pursuit can engender. I hope here to simply elucidate some issues to consider when thinking about college.

The Ratings Revenge

School counselors, private tutors, advisors, and parents have all become quite savvy in recent years about the college application process. You've seen the articles on whether to do fencing or crew, whether to take Latin or Spanish, whether to go to Costa Rica or Cozumel over spring break, and the impact these activities will have on a student's chances at this or that school. But the colleges have turned the tables and are playing the same game. Ever since *U.S. News and World Report* began to rank colleges, and parents began to pay attention to the number-one versus the number-seventeen school, colleges have realized that they have to work the numbers, too. Many colleges are making important strategic decisions based on the impact on their rankings. It's no longer "who is the best applicant to enroll in this specific class." The colleges now have their own agendas that do not necessarily hew to the merit-based, humane selection process that parents and students envision.

The "early decision" process is a good example of this change, as you've learned with your son. Once a process used to admit students who were certain in October of their senior year where they wanted to go to college; now it is a strategic move on the part of colleges to enhance selectivity and control financial aid. Many seniors are not quite ready to commit to a college but feel forced into participating in this process because they believe it enhances their chances.

The use of the Common Application and computer applications has dramatically increased the number of applications received by colleges and played into schools' efforts to improve their rankings. Why not send out a few more if all it takes is a click of the mouse? Maybe you'll get lucky. Schools like the flood of applications because it allows them to improve on their selectivity percentages and thus boost their overall rankings. If you can claim you reject 70 percent of the students who apply, you're more selective than a school that rejects only 40 percent. Harvard and Princeton's acceptance rates are now at record lows, hovering around 11 percent. Of course, this serves to further dehumanize the process and reduce it to a numbers exercise.

Competition Is Overwhelming

Last year more than 1.3 million high school seniors took the SAT 1. On the verbal section, more than 58,000 scored 700 or above, and on the math, more than 71,000 scored 700 or above. In one year in the early nineties, before competition became as intense as it is now, 2,669 students with SAT math scores between 750 and 800 applied to Princeton; 650, or only 24 percent, were accepted. Last year, Harvard turned down more than half its applicants with perfect SAT scores and 80 percent who were valedictorians. The applications director of Princeton once said memorably that he could throw out all the acceptances and find another, equally well-qualified freshman class in the rejected applicants.

The bottom line that students must understand is that college admission is not merit based: It takes terrific credentials to be considered by a top-notch college, but terrific credentials do not guarantee admission. In fact, as your son has painfully learned, the admissions process is idiosyncratic and often unfair. That's a simple fact.

I think it's important to resist the temptation to "take a shot" at top schools just on the chance your child will be admitted. Perhaps one or at the most two applications of this sort can be justified but when parents gamble that their child could "get lucky" the result is often a terribly demoralized student who is facing constant rejection. Teens don't understand taking this kind of risk: A rejection is a rejection to them, even if their parents knew that the chances were slim in the first place. Remember, too, that a child who gets admitted to a highly competitive school will be facing stiff competition for four years and may find himself in over his head if he's not prepared. Sometimes even guidance counselors are led astray; the numbers have become so overwhelming and the pressure so intense in the past couple of years, that even the professionals are getting blindsided.

Does Anyone Win the Applications Game?

Many parents and students do approach the whole idea of college admissions as a game. The hurdles are SATs, AP exams, the right extracurriculars, the best recommendations, impressive summer jobs, great athletics, and so on. Parents and students try to learn and manage the odds, often beginning in middle school. Will this prep school guarantee an automatic Ivy admit? Will a postgraduate year improve chances? Will an A+ in this course look better than a B in this more difficult course? How many hours of community service make sense? Some of this type of thinking is natural and inevitable. On the other hand, when it begins to affect the way families lead their lives, and when the focus becomes the goal—college—rather than the process—education—everyone suffers. Worse, if the goal is not reached, it seems that all was for naught.

When parents help to turn college acceptance into a strategy and a game, students come to understand that what really matters is fulfilling a parent's fantasy or winning a game, not appreciating and serving the child's needs.

Some misguided parents ratchet up the competitive levels, forcing other parents to make every effort to protect their child from unreasonable stress and pressure.

"The Right College Guarantees the Right Life"

Many parents have come to believe that only if their children get into the right school, will they find a good job, the best spouse, the right contacts, and their life will simply fall into place. They'll earn plenty of money and will be happy and successful. This impulse drives many parents to look to an Ivy diploma as the final top grade on their years of parenting. The actual facts—the real-life results of an Ivy education—are, as you might imagine, a subject that's been studied extensively. Is it worth it to go to a top school? Well, some studies have said that graduates of highly selective colleges do make more money. But it's not entirely due to their college diploma: They seem to be successful partly because their families are more affluent and better connected than average, and partly because they have strengths that would have helped them succeed at any college and, indeed, in any situation. A recent study by Stacy Berg Dale of the Andrew W. Mellon Foundation and Alan B. Krueger of Princeton revealed that among 1976 high school graduates accepted at both highly selective and moderately selective colleges, those attending the latter were actually earning slightly more than those who chose the top schools: an average of $91,200 in 1995 versus $90,100. (Students from lower-income families did significantly better after attending elite colleges.) Of course, it's a measure of our society that we try to assess the effects of a college education in solely financial terms. "Does a degree from an Ivy League college guarantee you a better income?" seems the wrong question. We should be asking instead what difference a degree from an Ivy League school would make in our lives. Or, rather, what difference does a good education, which can be had at any number of schools, have on one's life. An appropriate college for your child—one where he is challenged yet comfortable—can certainly change his life by exposing him to new ways of thinking, to the pleasures of our cultural and literary heritage, to the delights of intellectual discipline. If those goals take a more prominent place in parents' thinking, students will benefit and the process of college applications will become a more realistic exercise.

The Good News

With the bulge in the population of young people applying to colleges, schools have been in a position to improve on their student profiles and their academic standings. Schools that a few years ago were third-tier colleges are now moving up to second or first tier. As the caliber of students improves at many second- and third-tier schools, the intellectual atmosphere and quality of instruction also improves, and a school that ten years ago might have offered a lackluster experience can be a real find today.

One result of specialization and the trickle down of talent is that hyperselective schools are not the only ones with world-class programs. Geography is a school, not just a department, at Clark University in Worcester, Massachusetts; Harvard abolished its geography department decades ago. Rutgers has a whole school of communication and information studies; Princeton has no department in either field. Rensselaer Polytechnic is a leader in lighting studies, Virginia Tech in human-machine interaction; you won't find comparable programs at Cal Tech. While it's true that the most selective colleges offer more good elective courses and generally have better libraries and laboratories, even small rural schools can offer formidable numbers of online journals, thanks to the Internet.

Keep in mind that people change jobs and careers regularly in today's world. A college and major that might seem the perfect choice to a seventeen-year-old today may well be shed like a snake's skin in three years. Flexibility, enthusiasm, and a good work ethic are the qualities that spell success in today's world. Without these, even an Ivy diploma is no advantage.

Given what you've told me about your son's high school experience, I'm sure that he'll do well at any college he attends. Finally, remember that an education is its own reward.

Here are some books that you might find helpful:

- *Looking Beyond the Ivy League: Finding the College That's Right for You* by Loren Pope (Penguin Paperback, 1996)

- *Letting Go: A Parents' Guide to Understanding the College Years* by Karen Levin Coburn and Madge Lawrence Treeger (HarperPerennial Library, 3rd ed., 1997)

SOURCES

INTRODUCTION: THE WORLD OF ALMOST PERFECT

"Beating the Ivy League Odds," *Wall Street Journal,* April 16, 1999, p. W1.
"Beating the Ivy League Odds," *New York Observer,* April 16, 1999.
"The One Hundred Best High Schools" by Jay Mathews, 3/13/00, p. 50.

PART I: RESISTING THE HYPES THAT MAKE YOU PUSH

EVERYBODY'S DOING IT!
David Elkind, *Miseducation: The Preschooler at Risk.* New York: Knopf, 1987.

"Bill Johnson's Failed Comeback Was About More Than Glory," *New York Times,* April 6, 2001.

"Ease Up, Top Colleges Tell Stressed Applicants," Kate Zepnike, *New York Times,* December 7, 2000.

"For $300 an Hour, Advice on Courting Elite Schools," *New York Times,* October 25, 2000.

"Ivy League Fever," *New York Times,* September 24, 2000.

"Private School Squeeze," Kathleen Megan, *Hartford Courant,* April 5, 2000, p. B2.

"The Waiting Game," *Our Town,* Catherine Hausman and Victoria Goldman, February 7, 2000, p. 8.

NINE OUT OF TEN EXPERTS SAY SO!

Cyril Lodowic Burt, et al., *How the Mind Works.* New York: Books for Libraries Press, 1970.

Glenn Doman, *How To Teach Your Baby to Read: The Gentle Revolution,* New York: Avery Penguin Putnam, 1994.

David Elkind, *The Hurried Child.* Reading, Pa.: Addison-Wesley, 1985.

———. *Miseducation.* New York: Knopf, 1987.

Jean Grasso Fitzpatrick, *The Superbaby Syndrome: Escaping the Dangers of Hurrying Your Child.* San Diego: Harcourt Brace Jovanovich, 1988.

Jerome Kagan, *Three Seductive Ideas.* Cambridge: Harvard University Press, 1998.

Burton L. White, *The First Three Years of Life.* New York: Prentice Hall, 1978.

"Education of Babies Shown to Boost IQs," *San Francisco Chronicle,* February 10, 1991.

"From Better Babies to Better Learners?: Maybe," William Sharpe, *Wall Street Journal,* July 18, 2000, p. 1.

"The Mozart Effect," *Nature,* November 1993.

"The Nature of Emotion," Milt Klaus, *Time,* February 3, 1997, p. 46.

"The Quest for a Super Kid," *Time,* April 30, 2001.

"Trophy Kids," *Money,* March 1997.

You Can Manage It All!

David Brooks, *Bobos in Paradise*. New York: Simon and Schuster, 2000.

A. Freud, and D. Burlington, "War and Children," in *The World of the Child*, ed. Toby Talbot. New York: Jason Aronson, 1974.

"It's Not Big Brother Invading Kids' Privacy, It's Mom and Dad," *Wall Street Journal*, November 6, 2000.

"The Organization Kid," *Atlantic Monthly*, April 2001.

"The Parent Trap: Overworrying Small Risks, Ignoring Big Ones," *Wall Street Journal*, December 15, 2000.

"Tutor in Two-Wheel Independence," *New York Times*, September 24, 2000.

"The $28,995 Tutor," *New York*, April 16, 2001.

"You Can't Get Them Out with a Bomb," *Talk*, November 2000.

Money Equals Happiness

Mark Katy, *On Playing a Poor Hand Well*. New York: W. W. Norton, 1997.

David G. Meyers, *The Pursuit of Happiness: Discovering the Pathway to Fulfillment, Well-being and Enduring Personal Joy*. New York: Avon, 1993.

"Consumed by Consumerism," *Atlanta Journal-Constitution*, December 13, 1998.

"Don't Get the Wrong Message," Susan Faludi, *Newsweek*, January 8, 2001.

"Teenage Shoppers (Purses by the Brink)," Ruth La Fevla, *New York Times*, September 10, 2000.

Mirror, Mirror on the Wall, You're the Greatest Mom of All!

Bruno Bettelheim, *A Good Enough Parent*. New York: Vintage, 1988.

D. W. Winnicott, "Transitional Objects and Transitional Phenomena," in *Home Is Where We Start From*. New York: W. W. Norton, 1971.

"An American Family," *Wall Street Journal*, June 21, 1993.

"Children Often Pay the Price for Parents' Dreams," *San Francisco Chronicle*, April 12, 1996.

"The Contradictory Truths of 9 to 5," *New York Times*, April 25, 2001.

Almost Perfect

Peter Kramer, *Listening to Prozac: A Psychiatrist Explores Antidepressant Drugs and the Remaking of the Self.* New York: Penguin, 1997.

"Beyond Depression," *Time,* May 17, 1999.
"The Doubting Disease," *The New Yorker,* April 10, 2000.

PART II: THE FALLOUT OF PUSH PARENTING

The Pushed-Apart Family

"Changes in American Childrens' Time, 1981–1997," Hofferth, Sandra. University of Michigan Institute for Social Research, Center Survey, January 1999.

"Children Want Parents to Stop Making Plans and Start Hanging Out," *Wall Street Journal,* February 28, 2001.

"Overscheduled Families Discover a New Solution: Just Say 'No,' " *Wall Street Journal,* August 25, 2000.

"Talking with Teens: The YMCA Parent and Teen Survey," Global Strategy Group, Inc., Final Report, April 2000.

The Entitled, High-Maintenance Child

Maureen Stout, *The Feel-Good Curriculum: The Dumbing Down of America's Kids in the Name of Self-Esteem.* Cambridge: Perseus, 2001.

Daniel Goleman, *Emotional Intelligence.* New York: Bantam, 1997.

Alain De Bottom, *How Proust Can Change Your Life: Not a Novel.* New York: Vintage, 1998.

"The Age of Diminishing Innocence," *New York Times,* April 2, 2001.

"Elmo Gets Wired," *New York Times,* April 24, 2001.

"Summer Work Is Out of Favor with the Young," *New York Times,* June 18, 2000.

"The Truth About Tweens," *Newsweek,* October 18, 1999.

"You Can't Get Them Out with a Bomb," *Talk,* November 2000.

"Measuring Up for Ballet Class," Jennifer Dunning, *New York Times,* January 13, 2001, p. B23.

"The Evolution of Gift Giving," Cynthia Crossen, *Wall Street Journal,* November 27, 2000, p. B14.

MORAL BANKRUPTCY

Joan Jacobs Brumberg, *The Body Project: An Intimate History of American Girls.* New York: Random House, 1997.

Deborah Roffman, *Sex and Sensibility: The Thinking Parent's Guide to Talking Sense About Sex.* Cambridge: Perseus, 2000.

"Battling the Cheats," *New York Times,* November 20, 2000.

"The Cheating Game 'Everyone's Doing It from Grade School to Graduate School,'" *US News & World Report,* November 22, 1999.

"Dangerous Games: A Sex Video Broke the Rules, but for Kids, the Rules Have Changed," *Washington Post,* April 15, 2001.

Investigator Says Teachers in City Aided in Cheating," *New York Times,* December 9, 1999.

Rhode Island Rape Crisis Center Report: Reported by Jacqueline Jackson Kikuchi, staff member of the Rhode Island Rape Crisis Center, at the 1988 National Symposium on Child Victimization, Anaheim, Calif.

"Teens Seized in Human Torch Horror," *New York Post,* August 28, 1987.

"To Impress Colleges, Some Prep Schools Use Aggressive New Tactics," *Wall Street Journal,* January 23, 2001.

"The Truth About Tweens," *Newsweek,* October 18, 1999.

U.S. News poll, Lake Snell Perry & Assoc. and Tarrance Group, October 18–23, 1999.

THE BIG BACKFIRES: ANXIETY, INHIBITION, AND ADOLESCENCE

"The Case Against Competition," Alfie Kohn, *Working Mother,* September 1987, p. 32.

PART III: SOLVING THE PERPLEXING ISSUES

STRATEGIES
Social and Appearance Issues

American Society of Plastic Surgery, press release , April 9, 1999.
"The Epidemiology of Eating Problems in Nonreferred Children and Adolescents," *Child and Adolescent Psychiatry Clinics of North America,* vol. 2, no. 1, January 1993, pp. 1–13.

COLLEGE: THE END OF THE RAINBOW?
Loren Pope, *Looking Beyond the Ivy League: Finding the College That's Right for You.* New York: Penguin, 1996.
Karen Levin Coburn, and Madge Lawrence Treeger, *Letting Go: A Parent's Guide to Understanding the College Years.* New York: Harper, 1997.

"Estimating the Payoff to Attending Selective Colleges: An Application of Selection on Observables and Unobservables," NBER Working Paper no. W7322, August 1999.
"The New Safety Schools," by Elizabeth Bernstein 3/30/01 WKND.SECTION p. 1

ELISABETH GUTHRIE, M.D., is Clinical Director of the Learning Diagnostic Center at Blythedale Children's Hospital in Valhalla, New York. The mother of three children, she lives in Riverdale, New York.

KATHY MATTHEWS is the bestselling author of numerous books, including *The Savvy Mom's Guide to Medical Care,* which she coauthored with Dr. Pam Gallin. The mother of two sons, she lives in Pelham, New York.